Dressing with color

The Designer's Guide to over 1,000 Color Combinations

JEANNE ALLEN

IKUYOSHI SHIBUKAWA
and YUMI TAKAHASHI

CHRONICLE BOOKS
SAN FRANCISCO

Introduction

For many, the day-to-day dealings with a limited wardrobe can be a depressing and seemingly insurmountable problem. But in fact, putting together a wardrobe that works is a skill just like any other. You don't have to be a graduate of Seventh Avenue or have a highly leveraged wardrobe to look great. You can put it together yourself, for the most part from what you already own.

Dressing with Color presents a system that requires you to look at your wardrobe in a completely different way—not outfit by outfit or piece by piece but in color groups. By starting

with what you already own, you can recoordinate and add a few key pieces to build a custom wardrobe that is both efficient and a reflection of your personal style. If you find yourself being beaten down by a wardrobe that doesn't work, you can use this book to jog yourself into a new way of looking at old things. You may have racks of navy blue in your wardrobe (it *was* the great investment dressing color of the eighties), and you may have suits that never wear out. Take heart, turn to the navy section, consider mixing navy with white, pastels for Spring, or earth tones for Summer.

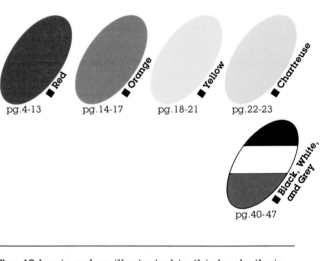

■ Red
pg. 4-13

■ Orange
pg. 14-17

■ Yellow
pg. 18-21

■ Chartreuse
pg. 22-23

■ Black, White, and Grey
pg. 40-47

The 49 basic colors illustrated in this book, their names, and page numbers.

Green pg.24-27	**Turquoise** pg.28-29	**Capri Blue** pg.30-31	**Royal Blue** pg.32-35	**Purple** pg.36-37	**Magenta** pg.38-39
Peach pg.48-53	**Powder** pg.54-55	**Cream** pg.56-57	**Aqua** pg.58-61	**French Blue** pg.62-63	**Periwinkle** pg.64-65
Claret pg.66-69	**Cocoa** pg.70-73	**Ochre** pg.74-75	**Malachite** pg.76-79	**Navy** pg.80-85	**Plum** pg.86-89
Beige pg.90-93	**Taupe** pg.94-97	**Brown** pg.98-101	**Carmel Brown** pg.102-103	**Khaki** pg.104-105	**Olive** pg.106-107

Red

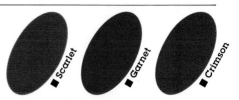

3 Variations of Red

Red is charged with passion and energy. We "see red" when angry, or "turn red" when embarrassed or over-emotional. Apart from metaphorical connotations, red's popularity in clothing is universal, spanning all ages and cultures. The power of red is such that even a red accent (a scarf, shoes, or a belt) can raise the most severe suit up from the depths of grimness.

Mixing Red with Basic Color Groups

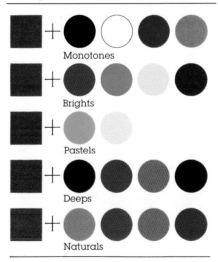

Monotones

Brights

Pastels

Deeps

Naturals

This color chart shows that both monotones and brights mix easily with red. Pastels are overwhelmed by red's vibrancy, so coordinates in this range have been left out. Color unions between red with naturals and red with deep jewel tones are tricky but effective if skillfully executed.

Red Alone: Scan these eight silhouettes, and you will quickly see which styles succeed and which fail when red is worn in its purest form. Clearly, the modern, simple shapes in figures 3 and 6 can sustain the vibrant color. The black accessories in fig-

ures 6, 7, and 8 balance the red and create a dramatic and sophisticated image. A red suit or a red raincoat may seem an unlikely wardrobe choice, but they will instantly brighten a dark, boring closet.

Red

Red with Monotones: Here we see how suits can be parlayed into a separates wardrobe that will take you from day into evening. Three suits in navy, red, and black-and-white plaid are the basic elements. Blazers in white and black and blouses in solids and stripes create additional options.

Figures 1–4 have a basic professional look suitable for any corporate environment, while figures 5–8 are more fashionable, with a longer, sleeker jacket worn over a short straight skirt. Both looks are professional, and their multiple mixing possibilities, an ideal choice for business travel.

Figures 1–4 show how the simple addition of a red blouse can enliven four monotone outfits. Because most professional wardrobes are based on a black, white, and grey color scheme, it is both easy and economical to begin to add color with

accessories. With key detail pieces, you can achieve the professional polish that ensures that you are getting the most from your suits and other expensive investment pieces.

Red

Red and Black Patterns: In these eight figures, red is mixed with greys and blacks in soft, sporty dressing that features bold woven patterns. The shapes are young and easy, making them a good match for the strong combination of design and color.

Again, the blazer is a key piece, shown here collarless in both solids and a red-and-black plaid. Turtleneck and zip-neck sweaters in knit, along with opaque stockings, are important accessories that help carry through this bold, contemporary look.

Red and White: Red, white, and blue or black is a never-fail color combination that is always in fashion. These colors are best used in easy sportswear looks like those in figures 1–4. You might already own some of the basic solid pieces here and be inspired to add a red-and-white plaid jacket or a striped T-shirt to expand your sportwear wardrobe. The skirt-blouse combination in figures 4-8 is rather boring stylewise but shows that you can't go wrong with this color mix, even when dots and abstract designs come into the picture.

Red

Red with Naturals: The outfits shown on this page and the next illustrate that a splash of red and a pinch of black will bring quick relief from the color tedium of brown or natural tones. Be warned, however, that red does not mix with natural colors as easily as with monotones and brights. Successful red-natural coordination is a matter of tone and amount. Rather than choosing a bright, clear red as we see here, find a red that is toned with brown, like the garnet red shown at the top of page 4. A deep red will lift the naturals without looking brash.

Red

The red-natural combination works best in casual soft looks that work best in Fall, but red combined with a khaki or olive cotton is popularly known as the "safari" or "military" look and is the year-round backbone of contemporary fashion stores such as

Banana Republic. These figures are more traditional and might be similar to some of the skirts, pants, or jackets that are lodged in your closet waiting for the kind of pick-me-up an injection of the right red can offer.

11

Red

Color Blocking Red with Brights: Color blocking, is an effective way to recycle sections of your wardrobe to create an upbeat and decidedly modern look. In figures 1–8, a relaxed silhouette composed of a V-neck sweater, a turtleneck, and a slim skirt is shown in a series of bold, contrasting color combinations. Although red dominates in each figure, the other colors balance the red because they are pure free-floating blocks of color devoid of patterning. Clearly some combinations are preferable, but color blocking can offer you some unexpected wardrobe options.

In figures 1–4, some patterning is introduced to break up the bright colors. This is
a more traditional way to mix red with
other brights, but these examples seem old
fashioned and dull compared to those on
the previous page. Figures 5–8 are more
interesting. High-voltage brights are mixed
together freely in figures 5 and 6. The red,
lime, purple, and orange combine well
because they share the same intense color
value. The addition of a bright print in figures 7 and 8 is fun and a good way to
expand on this casual summertime look.

13

Orange

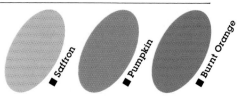

Saffron Pumpkin Burnt Orange

3 Variations of Orange

Not a color for the faint of heart, orange is strictly a fashion color that enjoys a surge of popularity every few decades. Its last big splash came in the sixties when its popularity surpassed even that of red. Orange is enjoying a modest revival now, but do not invest heavily in this color, no matter what the magazines say. You can, however, have some fun with a few carefully chosen pieces.

Mixing Orange with Basic Color Groups

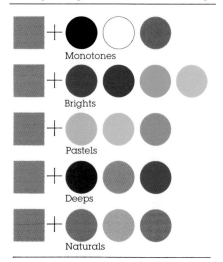

Monotones

Brights

Pastels

Deeps

Naturals

Orange works best as an accent color; it will not blend with other colors' unless they are from the same family. Orange as an accent will work with any of these color ranges except the pastels. Remember, however, that when it comes to orange, less is more.

Orange and Black: Although perfect for Halloween, steer your wardrobe clear of orange and black. If you like the idea of an ultramodern silhouette and a highly stylized fashion look, then trade the pure orange shown here for either the softer saffron color or the burnt orange color shown at the top of page 14. These two variations offer an opportunity to make a striking personal statement. Both saffron and burnt orange mix with black in a sophisticated, stylish way that works best in the kinds of dramatic silhouettes shown in figures 1, 2, 7, and 8.

15

Orange with Monotones: The heaviness of the black and orange combination in figures 1–4 is relieved when white is added. Pocket scarves in accent colors are introduced in figures 1 and 2, and a striped cotton pant and plaid jacket in figures 3 and 4 neutralize the impact of the eye-popping orange. Still, a better choice would be to replace the pure orange with either saffron or burnt orange. Even in the most skilled hands, orange tends to overwhelm monotones except when used in very small amounts.

Orange with Naturals and Brights: In figures 1–4, orange has been transformed into a mild bright by mixing it with naturals, creating a new and interesting aspect to a traditional and often stodgy color range. Injections of periwinkle blue in figure 2 and saffron in figures 3 and 4 accent this color story in just the right way. If you are inclined to go orange, this would be a sensible and tasteful route to take. In figures 5–8, orange is pitted against other brights, combinations that would have been everyday fare in the sixties but look awkward today. Orange is best used in a skirt or pants; worn near the face, orange will wash out even the most vibrant coloring.

17

Yellow

Marigold   Egg Yolk   Citron

3 Variations of Yellow

Yellow is a color that requires special handling. Almost everyone likes yellow—unlike orange, which is an acquired taste—but few people feel that they can wear it for any occasion other than active sports. It's easy to see why pure yellow is not taken seriously, but you can work marigold, egg yolk, or citron into your wardrobe without looking like Chiquita Banana.

Mixing Yellow with Basic Color Groups

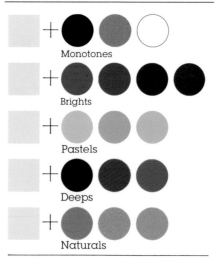

Monotones

Brights

Pastels

Deeps

Naturals

Yellow mixes best with monotones and brights. With pastels, yellow brings forth visions of Easter eggs and should therefore be avoided in those combinations. Yellow outshines the naturals. If you mix yellow with deep jewel tones, use marigold and practice restraint.

Yellow with Black and Grey: Figures 1–4 show yellow mixed with black for bold fashion dressing. While these outfits will no doubt play to mixed reviews, they are all quite acceptable for the occasions they suggest. Keep in mind, however, these are highly stylized looks that demand the sleek-

ness and vitality of youth to be successful. Anyone who opts for this color combination is seeking an audience who will stop and look. In figures 5–8, grey cannot stand up to the yellow and looks washed out even when white is introduced.

Yellow

Yellow with Black and White: Figures 1–4 combine yellow with white and use black, along with turquoise and bright pink, as accent colors. The plaids and stripes show that pattern and texture can be effective neutralizers when dealing with strong col- ors. Unlike some other combinations here, this is a bright, refreshing look with broad appeal. In figures 5–8, black and yellow are back in full force. The outfits shown are young and jazzy, featuring bold, graphic patterning and brightly colored accessories.

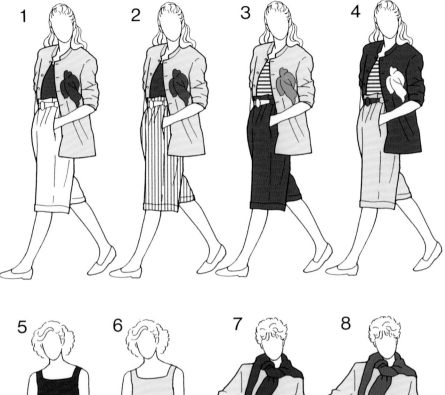

Yellow with Brights: Yellow and white mix effortlessly with blue in figures 1–4 to deliver an upbeat summertime sportswear look. This is a refreshing variation on the red, white, and blue nautical combinations that typify this kind of sporty dressing. In figures 5–8, citron yellow would be a more interesting choice than the pure yellow shown. With citron, both the bright and khaki combinations would have a sour bright look appropriate for these free and easy styles.

Chartreuse

2 Variations of Chartreuse

Mixing Chartreuse with Basic Color Groups

Monotones

Brights

Pastels

Deeps

Naturals

Chartreuse, like orange, lies dormant for years and then bursts upon the scene with a frightening energy. In reports on the 1991 Spring runway shows in New York, *Women's Wear Daily* complained of the visual exhaustion caused by viewing an endless parade of chartreuse and lime green garments. A year before, this color was seen only in swimsuits and bicycle clothes.

Chartreuse is often paired with black (creating an acceptable look in most circles). The downside is that both chartreuse and lime are cruel and unforgiving colors. The addition of black in figures 1 and 3 intensifies this tendency and shows a sharp, insistent image complimentary to very few of us. The addition of white can soften this impression easily. In figure 2, chartreuse and white are successfully combined into a warm-weather look. In figure 4, the chartreuse is limited to a soft, simple sweater tucked into a black-and-white check pant. This last silhouette is fashionable in the best sense of the word.

Chartreuse is an accessory in itself, something immediate to bring fun and newness to your off-time and weekend wardrobe. In figures 1–8, chartreuse is mixed with brights. In most cases, vivids are added to the basic lime and monotone theme set up on the previous page. Chartreuse works with the tertiary colors of purple, magenta, and orange, which share a common visual intensity. Brown can be used to soften the impact, particularly in tropical or ethnic prints.

Green

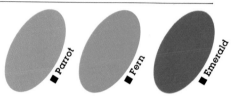

3 Variations of Green

This pure and vivid form of green, never as popular as bright red or bright blue, produces sallow complexions and is therefore considered a difficult color to wear. Any fashion designer who invests much of their collection in this color does so at great risk, but don't count green out. Many of the combinations here are bright and refreshingly different.

Mixing Green with Basic Color Groups

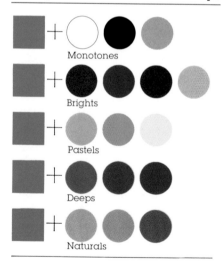

Green's dominating personality will draw and hold the viewer's eye, so it must be balanced with colors that enhance its clarity. Although it mixes effortlessly with monotones, brights, and certain jewel colors, green defies both naturals and pastels, so don't force the issue.

Green with White and Black: The first four figures have the freshness that we associate with green and white. This is an important color combination for resortwear. Green takes to the clean, natural personality of cotton and shines in the abstract print in figure 2, where a touch of red, green's complement, has been introduced to amplify green's clarity. Green and black is a more difficult combination to get right. Figures 7 and 8 have a vivacious chic completed with the addition of black stockings.

Typical Coordination with Green and Red:
In the top four figures, green is balanced almost evenly with red. Black and white are brought in to neutralize this intense color combination, and stripes are added as a visual element to ensure the casual, almost sporty mood of all these outfits. Strong geo-metrics are introduced in figures 6-8, and bright colors other than red are added in figures 5–8, suggesting that this is a good way to use green. This marginally unorthodox color combination of brights syncs perfectly with green's offbeat personality.

Purple and green are good friends. There is an affinity between the two colors that brings out the best in each. Figures 1–4 show several shades of purple, from violet to magenta, with green. In figure 3, a neutral blouse is successfully added; in fig-

ure 4, the juxtaposition of jewel brights sparks a conservative outfit. In figures 5–8, the throwaway mixes of candy color nearly reduce green to a neutral. Notice in these combinations that green no longer dominates any of the outfits.

Turquoise

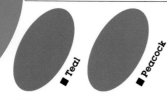

2 Variations of Turquoise

■ Teal ■ Peacock

Mixing Turquoise with Basic Color Groups

+ Monotones

+ Brights

+ Pastels

+ Deeps

+ Naturals

The color turquoise takes its name from the stone made up of varying amounts of blue and green. Having been admired for eons in Turkey, China, Arabia, India, and Mexico, this color was relatively rare in the U.S., except the Southwest, until recently. Turquoise today is an important part of every wardrobe. Like red, it can be sporty and dressy, depending on the colors combined with it.

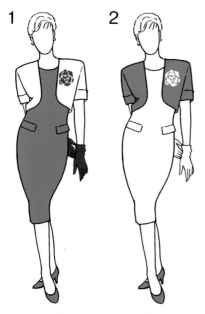

1   2   3   4

Turquoise with Monotones: In the Southwest, we usually see turquoise mixed with monotones. White and turquoise produce a clean, cool look, while black or grey with turquoise is dramatic. The simplicity of the shapes in figures 1–4 is accentuated with an equally simple color statement. In figure 1, a touch of violet provides an interesting counterpoint to the turquoise-and-white combination, but simple silver jewelry or accessories best complete this color scheme.

Two Sides of Turquoise: Turquoise used to be relegated to the kind of resortwear combinations shown in figures 5–8. Today, it is an acceptable color for the office, although figures 1–4 show that pairing turquoise with neutrals can be awkward. In figures 1, 2, and 4, the turquoise dominates the outfits and creates a harsh, almost institutional look. The intensity of the colors in figure 3 contributes to its balanced, professional image. Turquoise is clearly at home in figures 5–8 with the paintbox mixture of brights and white. Neutrals bring a sophisticated ease to these outfits.

Capri Blue

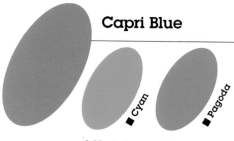

■ Cyan　■ Pagoda

2 Variations of Capri Blue

Mixing Capri Blue with Basic Color Groups

+ Monotones

+ Brights

+ Pastels

+ Deeps

+ Naturals

A jazzy color that looks good on almost everyone, capri blue may not enjoy the widespread popularity of turquoise, but in warm climates it can be counted on to project a cool, sporty image. A jolt of this brilliant clear color can breathe new life into a safe but tired wardrobe of monotones and brights, so don't be surprised if it attracts attention.

1   2   3   4

Capri Blue with Monotones: To add a dash of color to a basically black-and-white wardrobe, you might ordinarily use red or royal blue. You can't go wrong sticking to the tried and true, but you might try capri blue as a slightly off-beat alternative. In figures 1–4, capri

blue combines easily with either black or white. The addition of a few key capri blue pieces to the black and white basics hanging in every closet can create an inexpensive warm weather wardrobe. To add polish to this new look, invest in some dramatic pieces of silver jewelry.

Capri Blue with Bright, Pastel, and Deep Colors: In figures 1 and 2, black and white are used effectively as accent colors and bring a precision and sharpness to these sporty combinations. Figures 3 and 4 fall flat in comparison; the white is meant to balance the brilliant blue but succeeds only in looking dull. The vivacious brights are clearly the best choice. Figures 5 and 6 show unlikely but successful combinations of color. Tone and amount of color are perfectly balanced. Figures 7 and 8 are also unorthodox but don't work very well.

Royal Blue

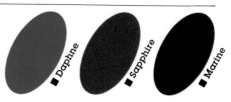

3 Variations of Royal Blue

This easy-to-wear, easy-to-coordinate all-American color is an across-the-board favorite. This clean, clear blue has such sure sale appeal that most designers have a group of colors built around royal blue to open their Spring season. For most people, this color is a wardrobe anchor. Since you probably already own a royal skirt, jacket, dress, or sweater, here are some new ways to use this color.

Mixing Royal Blue with Basic Color Groups

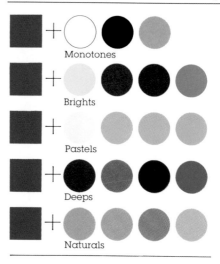

Monotones

Brights

Pastels

Deeps

Naturals

Most people will say that blue is their favorite color, and this shade of royal is their favorite blue. There are countless opportunities to see royal every day because it can be worn on its own, mixed with basic monotones, or combined with other clear brights.

Royal Blue with Whites: Royal's first mate is white, and the combination is faultless, whatever the style. Figures 3 and 4 are clearly inspired by the classic sailor suit. Figures 5–8 show different knit fabrics designed to create modern, versatile sportswear styles. In figures 5 and 6,

Lycra—a stretchy cotton knit—is used to make the kind of body-hugging dresses that appeal to the young and lithe. Figures 7 and 8 also show knits that can be worn easily by anyone, particularly the not-so-young and not-so-lithe.

Royal Blue with Brights: Bright yellow is at its best when added to royal and white. The nautical theme, the look is now brighter and more sporty. White is used in measured amounts to keep the yellow and royal balanced in figures 1–3. In figure 4, yellow and royal are used in a strong graphic in which the dress resembles a semaphore flag. The first three styles are much easier to understand and wear. In figures 5–8, yellow is replaced by red in a traditional tricolor combination. These four figures show that when it comes to red, white, and blue, style is never limited by color.

Royal Blue with Other Brights: Royal assumes a different character when balanced with a mixture of other brights. With orange and yellow, royal becomes deep and cool, emphasizing the sunshine intensity of the warm colors. In figure 2, royal melds with pastels and hot pink, creating an unusual but interesting combination. Figures 3 and 4 also offer unlikely combinations that somehow work. Things become simpler in figures 5–8. Black encourages the drama and intensity of the royal in figure 5.

Purple

■ Mulberry   ■ Heliotrope

2 Variations of Purple

Purple was once the color of emperors and popes, and for good reason. The dye required to make the rich, deep color was so expensive that only a few could afford the precious purple textiles. Even when the dyes became affordable, the wearing of purple was often restricted by law to the aristocracy. Today, everyone wears purple, but it remains a special color that carries a strong emotional charge.

Mixing Purple with Basic Color Groups

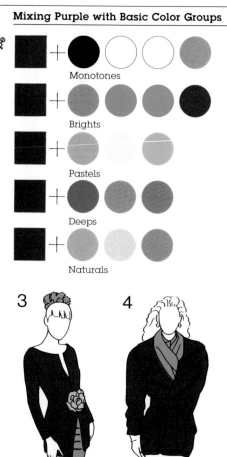

Monotones

Brights

Pastels

Deeps

Naturals

1   2   3   4

Purple with Monotones: Purple is considered more elegant and unusual than blue, so it is often mixed with monotones when a sophisticated or dressy look is required (figure 1). Purple and grey have become a popular combination recently, particularly in professional dressing, where restraint and subtlety are a necessity. Figures 2

and 3 show purple-grey, but the styles are too frivolous for this serious color combination. Purple and white are usually worn together in Spring and Summer, but the mix in figure 4 works well for Fall. The potential bleakness of the combination is avoided by the addition of a wooly turquoise scarf.

Purple and Unusual Contrasts: Purple can be combined with monotones and brights to achieve conventional looks, yet its exotic nature can be brought out by mixing it with acrid and vegetable colors. In figures 1–4, purple is mixed with green, orange, and turquoise. These combinations may not be for everyone, but they have definite merits. Purple is often paired with difficult colors (figures 3 and 4) with good results. In figures 5–8, it is clear that purple can be stretched only so far. These are bizarre color combinations that should be avoided.

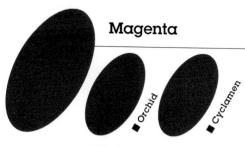

Magenta

■ Orchid   ■ Cyclamen

2 Variations of Magenta

Mixing Magenta with Basic Color Groups

+ ● ○ ● Monotones

+ ● ● ● ● Brights

+ ● ● ● Pastels

+ ● ● ● Deeps

+ ● ● ● ● Naturals

Flamboyant magenta is most successful as an accent but appears everywhere now from couture to beachwear. Like purple, it combines well with monotones, brights, and spicy colors, making it a versatile mixer. Some magenta hints: 1) a little goes a long way, 2) keep it away from your face. Otherwise, have fun with this hot color that offers both spice and style.

1   2   3   4

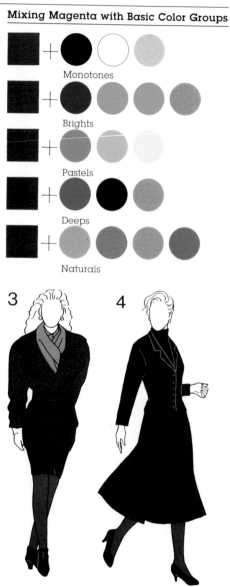

Magenta is often mixed with monotones, particularly black, and is a good vehicle for expanding your basic black, white, and grey wardrobe. Magenta and black together are regarded as a sophisticated combination and, because of this, are often used for eveningwear (figure 1). The down side of this combination is that it can be very cold and harsh, so either add a softening color like the camel scarf in figure 3 or wear the magenta away from your face (figure 4). Magenta is sometimes paired with grey, but this works only when a soft magenta is used. The real thing tends to overwhelm any color that lacks deep saturation.

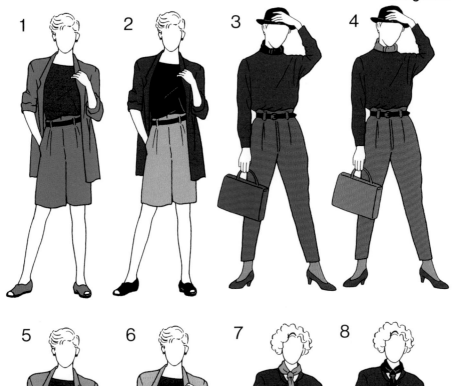

Magenta is very versatile. Like purple, it enhances the green in figure 1. The pairing of magenta with beige in figure 2 is unsuccessful for the same reasons magenta fails with grey. Magenta is delicious with spice colors like the orange in figure 5 and the saffron jacket in figure 6. The beige jacket in figure 5 is a mistake, but the magenta, purple, turquoise combination in figure 8 is one of the most popular combinations in fashion today. Note that in all of these figures the magenta is kept away from the face with a scarf or a jacket.

Black, White, and Grey

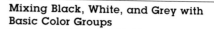

Variations of White, Grey, and Black

Black-and-white has always stood for urban smartness. Black-and-white began its ascendancy as the definitive color scheme of choice and convenience for the professional woman in the seventies. A wardrobe based on black and white is easy to coordinate, easy to travel with, and can be taken from daytime into evening with only minor accessory changes.

Mixing Black, White, and Grey with Basic Color Groups

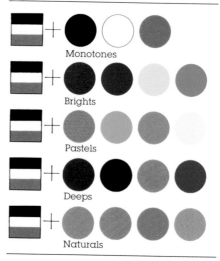

Black-and-white coordinates with other monotones especially well when one of the colors is in a pattern or plaid. Brights breathe life into black-and-white. Naturals are less likely to mix well—the urbanity of the black-and-white conflicts with the fragile personality of soft browns and beiges.

The visual simplicity of black-and-white allows a pattern mixing that might well be tasteless in living color. Four graphic combinations are shown in figures 1–4. Figure 2 shows a black-on-white check jacket paired with a skirt in a miniature version of the jacket pattern. This kind of coupling is called "paired patterns." For a change of pace, black and white are used in opposition in figures 5–8, with dramatic effect. A bright accent color relieves the severity of the combination. Red is the most popular accent for black-and-white, but the violet in figure 5 is the winner for an evening accent.

Black, White, and Grey

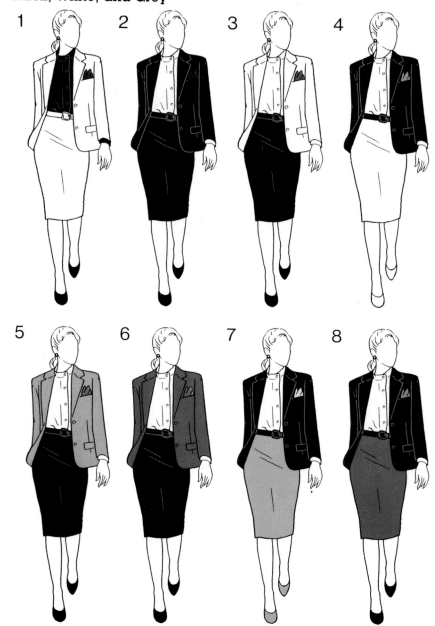

This kind of professional dressing may appear to be failsafe, but be aware of some pitfalls. First, this is investment dressing—the fabric and the tailoring should be impeccable. The two pieces of the suit must be cut from the same cloth if they are ever to be worn together. Second, if you wear the two pieces separately with other items, make sure that one doesn't look more worn than the other. Third, choose a blouse in a contrasting color. Figure 4 shows a white blouse with a white skirt, but these whites will never match unless they were cut from the same bolt of fabric.

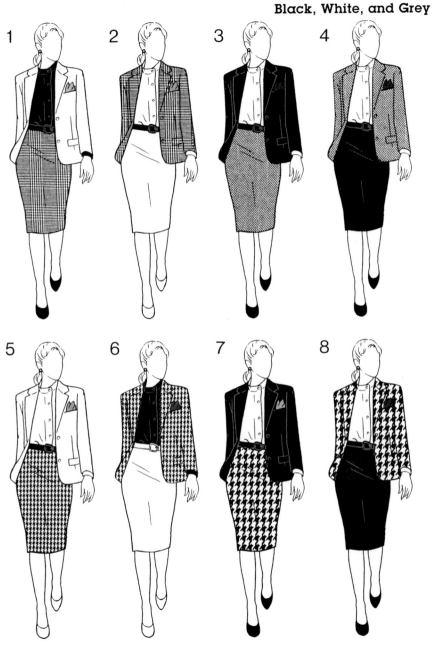

In figures 1–8, the corporate look is translated into black-and-white wovens. Figures 1 and 2 show a matched plaid in combination with a white suit. Again, good quality is important. This type of plaid must be matched, a laborious and time-consuming tailoring process that is reflected in the price. In figures 3 and 4, a conservative herringbone skirt is worn with a black suit jacket. Figures 5–8 show varying sizes of houndstooth checks, a more casual look that is popular for Spring dressing.

Black, White, and Grey

One sure sign of Spring is the appearance of black and white polka dots. In figures 1–4, swingy, cinch-waisted skirts are topped with feminine, short-sleeved blouses. Again, watch for matching in figures 1 and 4. On the page, the solid blouses match the ground color of the skirt; in reality, a piece of dyed fabric (solid) and a printed fabric (dots) will never match exactly. Stripes take over in figures 5–8. Bold horizontal stripes (figures 7 and 8) are reserved for the perfectly proportioned in either a dress or a two-piece suit.

These figures show three-piece coordination in black and white using a variety of shapes and textures. The styling in figures 1 and 2 is kept modern with the simple turtle-neck sweater under the spencer jacket. A delicate lattice plaid is used in the jacket of figure 1, a larger plaid in the skirt of figure

2. The younger look in figure 3 comes from shortening the flared skirt and exchanging the jacket for a plaid vest. The black vest and turtleneck in figure 4 balance the black-and-white abstract print in the skirt. The styling in figures 5–8 becomes softer and more sophisticated.

Black, White, and Grey

The easiest way to expand and renew your black-and-white wardrobe is to add a splash of color. In figure 1, green and red accents perk up the white jacket. A blast of orange wakes up figure 2's sophisticated but potentially severe ensemble. Figures 3 and 4 show that bright color can be a posi-tive addition to black-and-white patterns. The success of the pastel combinations in figures 5–8 owes much to the sophisticated This kind of unusual but carefully orches-trated coordination can invigorate and renew a rather tired wardrobe.

The blocks of deep, rich color in figures 1–8 are balanced against black and grey. The result is concise but highly personal. Each of the eight figures is styled in an elegant and professional way. Black or grey is used as the basic here, but both color and pat-tern bring in sufficient diversity to ensure that each of the stylings is completely different. The pivotal styling element here is the blouse or sweater. With a change in color or pattern, or with the addition of a belt, the image will change totally.

Peach

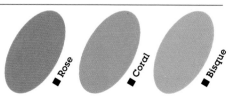

3 Variations of Peach

Peach is a cosmetic color that can be either sophisticated or insipid, depending on how it is used. Peach is a beauty color, delicate and subtle, so it must be handled with care. The key to using peach correctly is in acknowledging its frailty and coordinating it to enhance the warmth and softness of the color.

Mixing Peach with Basic Color Groups

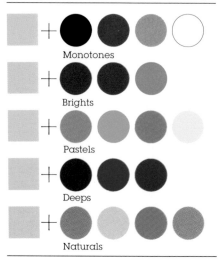

Monotones

Brights

Pastels

Deeps

Naturals

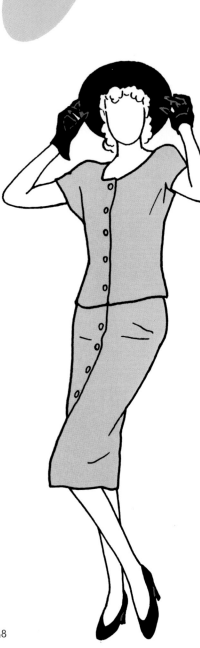

Peach is dramatic when mixed with monotones, provocatively subtle when combined with the deep, dark colors of navy, brown, and purple, and sophisticated as an accent used with neutrals. Don't use peach in large amounts; a touch here and there is quite enough.

Here are eight distinctive looks styled in various peach and black combinations. Peach works equally well as a top or a bottom in solid, woven, or print. The first three figures show dressed-up looks that might be fabricated in silk and crepe combinations.

Figures 4 and 5 are casual, showing peach in spotted and plaid designs. In figures 6 and 7, peach and black are combined to present a more professional look; in outfit 8, they are juxtaposed as color-blocked solids with black accessories.

Peach

Figures 1–4 show peach as either a jacket or a blouse in combination with other pieces in navy, white, and black-white plaid. In figures 5–8, peach is matched with similar colors, but the styling is more casual, show-ing how versatile this color is. Peach is young and spirited when mixed with black-and-white stripes and plaids. Throughout all of these combinations, white is used consis-tently to keep the peach fresh and light.

In figures 1–4, peach is combined with soft grey. Once again, white is used to freshen the look. Peach alone or peach with white might be too sweet a combination, but the soft grey introduces a sophistication without sacrificing the femininity of the colors. The soft grey in figures 6 and 7 creates a look with a little more edge than the previous combinations. The blue, white, and peach outfits in figures 5–8 are an unusual way to combine blue and white. The peach is a nice change from the expected red or yellow.

Peach

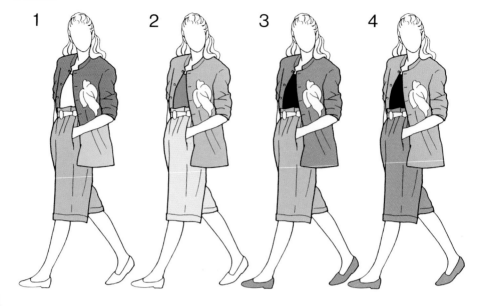

In the first four casual combinations, white is used as an effective accent. Figures 1 and 2 show peach with other pastels—a lavender and a soft yellow. In figures 3 and 4, black and grey act as a well-balanced counterpoint to the peach. In the last four figures, white is replaced with a bright color. Here, peach is expected to act as a neutral. The success of this attempt is marginal, particularly in figures 5 and 8, where the green causes the peach to behave aggressively.

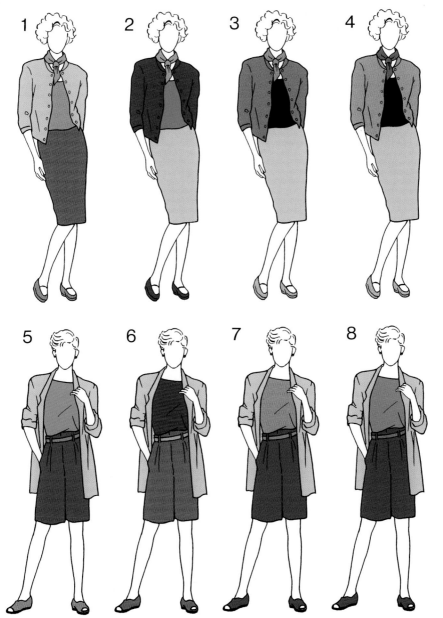

Figures 1–4 combine peach with neutral and natural colors. The main problem here is one of amount; there is too much peach for these slight colors. If peach is used as an accent, say in the scarf or the pullover top, it would invigorate the combination instead of overwhelming it. Figures 5–8, where soft colors are worn under a soft peach blazer, have the same problem. There is too much peach suffocating the other subtle colors.

Powder

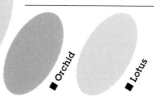

2 Variations of Powder

■Orchid ■Lotus

Mixing Powder with Basic Color Groups

Monotones

Brights

Pastels

Deeps

Naturals

This delicate color is often overlooked in favor of brighter pinks, but this shade is actually easier to coordinate with other colors than its rosy sisters. Powder has a pale, dusty cast that makes it combine well with monotones and neutrals. A good accent color with charcoals and browns, powder works best with cool colors and should be kept away from vivid brights and warm pastels.

1 2 3 4

These four figures show a variety of styles, from outerwear to a three-piece knit set. In each case, the color combination is sophisticated and appropriate for its styling. The powder blazer over a navy skirt in figure 3 is a slightly unusual but excellent way to bring Spring color into the office without sacrificing professional demeanor. White is an important element in the first three figures. It keeps the outfits fresh and encourages the powder to act as a neutral rather than a pastel.

Grey is the color of choice with powder in figures 1–4. White and black act as important accents to create an edge to these outfits. It's evident that powder can be worn for any occasion, providing the color combination and balance are correct. Figures

5–8 show a more frivolous look, complete with a dyed-to-match hat. Powder has been worked in a series of eclectic, somewhat disturbing color combinations, the most successful being figure 5, where an overdose of powder is neutralized with other soft colors.

Cream

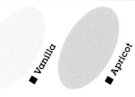

■ Vanilla ■ Apricot

2 Variations of Cream

Mixing Cream with Basic Color Groups

+ Monotones

+ Brights

+ Pastels

+ Deeps

+ Naturals

Cream is softer and easier to wear than a true yellow. It combines best with monotones and naturals, but is often worn with other pastels or as a substitute for yellow with brights. A Spring color that can be worn into Summer, cream is rarely seen in the Fall except as an accent. It has a longer reach than pink or blue and can be very nice simply worn on its own.

1 2 3 4

Cream is combined with black, white, navy, and grey in figures 1–4. Cream can also be used successfully on its own or mixed with pure white. The white in these four figures keeps them fresh and light. The black, cream, and white outfits in figures 1 and 2 are sharp with a put-together look. A pocket scarf in aqua and a neck scarf in violet provide a nice accent. Figure 3 shows the affinity between grey and cream. Cream is good with navy and is shown here in a three-piece, decidedly corporate look.

Figures 1–3 mix cream with monotones and soft pastels. The saccharine image often created when different pastels are worn together is avoided by adding grey or white. In figure 4, cream steps in for white, making a nice combination with turquoise and black. In figures 5 and 6, cream is mixed with bright colors with marginal success. The brightness of the turquoise and orange flatten cream, leaving the combination with an awkward look. The neutrals and other soft colors in figures 7 and 8 evoke a beautiful, romantic image.

Aqua

Sky ■   Delphinium ■   Teal ■

3 Variations of Aqua

Softer than turquoise but stronger than a true pastel, aqua looks good on everyone regardless of skin tone or age. This refreshing, breezy color is especially popular for Spring and Summer and is a particular favorite for active sportswear. Aqua is often paired with white for tenniswear and black or brights for swim and skiwear.

Mixing Aqua with Basic Color Groups

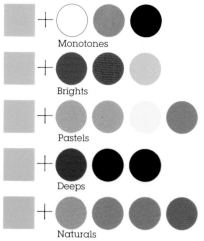

Monotones

Brights

Pastels

Deeps

Naturals

Aqua combines effortlessly with all the monotones. It creates a clean, fresh image with white, gives a spark to greys, and delivers a dramatic Summer look with black. A little aqua goes a long way with monotones, so use it as an accent with these colors.

Aqua is a favorite color choice for resort-wear. Figure 2 mixes aqua with two shades of grey, an unlikely mix considering the styling, but it shows how well aqua mixes with any grey. The look in figure 4 is especially popular for aerobic wear. Figures 5–8 show four looks suitable for the office and illustrate the flexibility of these color combinations. In figure 5, the colors are perfectly balanced between aqua and white, with a small black pocket scarf as an important accent. The aqua blouse in figures 6 and 7 provides a lift for these otherwise rather serious grey suits.

Aqua

Figures 1–4 combine aqua and white or aqua and black with a neutral color. In the first two figures, aqua is fabricated in either the skirt or the jacket while the blouses are white. These combinations are less successful than figures 3 and 4, where aqua is retained only as an accent in the blouse. Figures 3 and 4 are more sophisticated than the first two because they use the aqua to lighten the styling. In figures 5–8, aqua is again paired with either white or black, but here a stronger color is brought in as a third.

Aqua is at home with other pastels and soft brights on this page. In figures 1 and 2, white keeps the outfits from becoming too sweet. In figures 3 and 4, a color edge is created when the feminine quality of the soft colors is set in opposition to the black. The color mixes in figures 5 and 6 are tonally balanced, with grey acting as a neutral. Figures 7 and 8 combine aqua with navy and yellow orange, strong colors that leave aqua looking flat and anemic. There is too much aqua in these last figures; it would do better as an accent.

French Blue

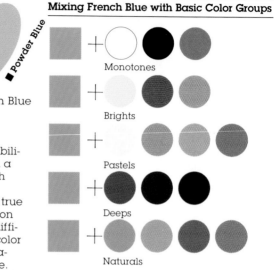

2 Variations of French Blue

Mixing French Blue with Basic Color Groups

Monotones

Brights

Pastels

Deeps

Naturals

The appeal of French blue is its ability to successfully coordinate with a variety of dissimilar colors. French blue behaves like a neutral but retains the softness of a pastel. A true pastel blue has a strong connection to the juvenile world, making it difficult to seriously consider such a color for an adult wardrobe; for this reason, French blue is a better choice.

French blue mixes gracefully with monotones, soft brights, and neutrals. The combinations on these pages that emphasize grey and white bring out the best in French blue—a good example to follow in considering how best to use this color. The first three figures use

French blue judiciously, with white, grey, or charcoal. These images project a cool, fresh image that is casual but contained. In figure 4, where a pink cardigan is added to offer a pastel image, the look is suburban compared to the color scheme in figure 3.

In these four figures, French blue is mixed with soft brights and tempered with accents of white and black. The black plaid that decorates the jacket in the first two figures brings a whole new personality to the blue color. Black imparts a sophistication. In fig-ures 5–8, blue is kept cool as it is mixed with cool beiges and greys—an interesting color concept. The French blue becomes the bright point in this rather droll color scheme.

Periwinkle

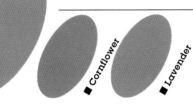

2 Variations of Periwinkle

Mixing Periwinkle with Basic Color Groups

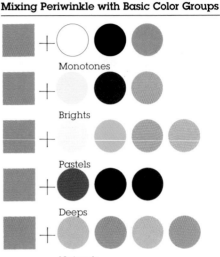

Monotones

Brights

Pastels

Deeps

Naturals

Periwinkle is a mild blue with a distinctive lavender cast, a beautiful, easy-to-wear color that just as easily combines with monotones, brights, and other pastels. Periwinkle can be a striking accent to naturals and deep brights. This seemingly innocuous color is surprisingly good with brown because it encourages the depth and richness of this sometimes difficult shade.

Figures 1–4 show periwinkle with grey, white, and black. The outfit in figure 1 featuring nautical stripes and a sailor hat illustrates the popularity of the peri/white combination for resortwear. Note that in figure 2, the black encourages the lavender side of periwinkle's character, resulting in a fresh, sophisticated image. The peri jacket worn over a charcoal grey dress in figure 3 is an unusual but appropriate professional look—the touch of pink provides a welcome lightness. In figure 4, periwinkle becomes the accent as a blouse worn with a pale grey suit. This combination is a direct lift from menswear but works nicely for women.

In figures 1 and 2, periwinkle is color-blocked with black, white, and grey. The pale pink cardigan in figure 2 re-emphasizes the strength of the peri, grey, pink triad. In both outfits, the color scheme is kept cool by using grey and black to ensure that the lighter colors never become saccharine. In figures 3 and 4, the peri shirt is styled in a casual way with natural colors. This easy-going feeling is continued in figures 5–8 with a straight periwinkle skirt worn with sweaters in soft brights. Black, white, and grey are used again as the astringent for the pastels. These combinations look haphazard but succeed by creating a refreshing, slightly unorthodox look.

Claret

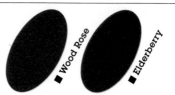

2 Variations of Claret

Wood Rose

Elderberry

A deep, noble color that embodies the rich traditions of Fall, claret is usually used in such luxurious materials as velvet, wool, silk, and leather. Because claret is a mix of browns, purples, and reds, it combines beautifully with these autumn colors and can be renewed by mixing it with any of its components.

Mixing Claret with Basic Color Groups

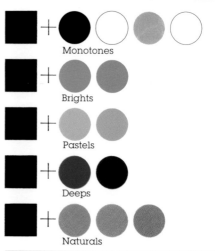

Monotones

Brights

Pastels

Deeps

Naturals

Claret combines with some monotones but should be kept away from light colors, pastels, and brights. Claret mixes with spice colors and dark jewel tones to create unusual, elegant combinations. Neutral colors tend to encourage claret's richness, making it appear more red.

Claret for Both Evening and Work: The evening ensemble in figure 1 is accented with a pink flower, providing a contrast color necessary to enhance the claret. In figures 2 and 3, black draws out the depth and richness of claret, making it an excellent choice for Fall and Winter evening dressing. The claret-and-white pairings in figure 4 should be avoided—neither color does anything to improve the other. Although there is nothing wrong with the combinations in figures 5–8, they seen uninspired and almost institutional.

Claret and Black Separates: In figures 1 and 2, claret and black are color-blocked (blocks of color stacked atop one another). In these dark colors, this simple look may be too severe for some, so the patterning in figures 3 and 4 provides a way to soften the combination. Adding an accessory (figures 5 and 6) can also soften and expand the black-claret combination. Grey and beige are added as third colors in figures 7 and 8 to create a more traditional and reserved look than in figures 5 and 6.

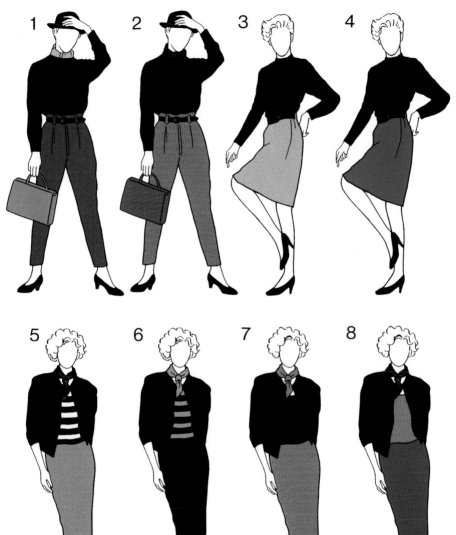

Claret with Neutrals, Navy, and Green:
Figures 1-8 sell short claret's versatility as a mixing color. Claret of course combines easily with soft neutrals, including the tan, grey, and charcoal separates in figures 1–3. But beyond these safe combinations, claret has an affinity for spice and jewel colors, such as saffron, pomegranate, violet, emerald, and indigo. Combinations using brighter colors (malachite and navy) in figures 4–8 are kept cool and reserved by adding soft neutrals.

Cocoa

3 Variations of Cocoa

Not long ago, basic brown was just that—the foundation of the autumn wardrobe. Sometime in the sixties, brown lost ground to more dramatic and exciting colors, such as black, claret, and royal blue. But this deep neutral version called cocoa might push brown back into the limelight. It can be as dramatic as black, without the sharpness and without being a fashion cliche.

Mixing Cocoa with Basic Color Groups

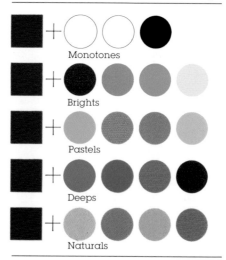

Monotones

Brights

Pastels

Deeps

Naturals

Cocoa is wasted on monotones. It approximates black in the way it works and consequently can be mixed with white or grey, but it works best with pastels, brights, and jewel tones. Cocoa mixes easily with neutrals, but it longs for a third color to complete the combination.

Cocoa with Soft Colors: In figures 1–4, neutrals tan, taupe, and dove are mixed conservatively with the cocoa. Pastels are introduced as blouses to relieve the severity of the combination without sacrificing the professional edge. In figures 5 and 6, a warm buttery brown pulls out the deep richness of the cocoa. The chalky pastels in figures 7 and 8 offer an unusual but striking contrast to cocoa.

Cocoa

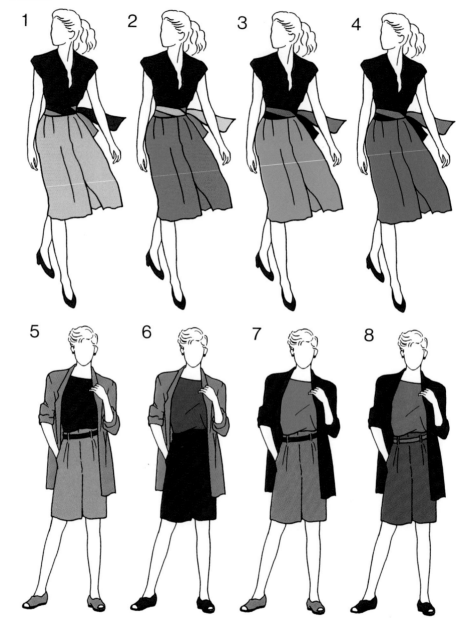

Cocoa with Brights: Tropical and ethnic prints often use cocoa as a component color, mixing it with a range of off-the-wall brights. But here in figures 1–4, cocoa is shown as a separate entity as a small summer top over a series of bright billowy skirts tied with multicolored sashes. In figures 5–8, where cocoa is mixed with neutrals and balanced with soft brights and eclectic pales, the look is casual yet sophisticated.

Cocoa with Pastels: The cocoa-pastel combinations in figures 1–4 are a natural for Spring dressing in mixtures of linen and knit. White works with this color combination, but the kinds of neutrals shown in figures 3 and 4 are more interesting. In figures 5 and 6, cocoa is paired with bright brights with disastrous results. The vivid red and green leave the cocoa brown looking drab and worn out. Figures 7 and 8 are only marginally better.

Ochre

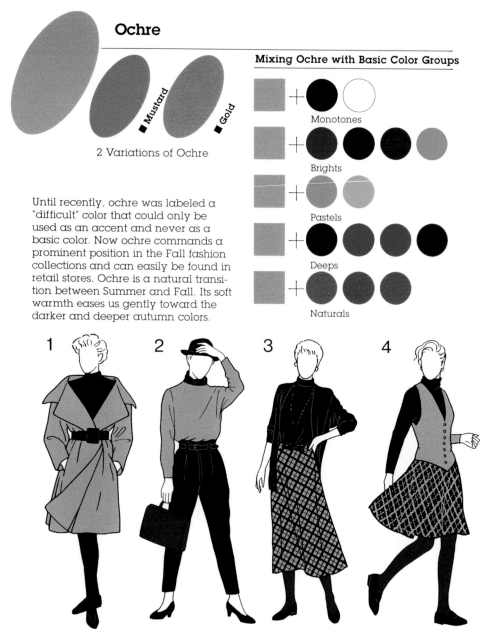

2 Variations of Ochre

■ Mustard   ■ Gold

Mixing Ochre with Basic Color Groups

Monotones

Brights

Pastels

Deeps

Naturals

Until recently, ochre was labeled a "difficult" color that could only be used as an accent and never as a basic color. Now ochre commands a prominent position in the Fall fashion collections and can easily be found in retail stores. Ochre is a natural transition between Summer and Fall. Its soft warmth eases us gently toward the darker and deeper autumn colors.

1   2   3   4

Ochre was once mixed exclusively with neutrals, making for a limited and rather boring color range. Here, ochre is mixed with black, brights, neutrals, and jewel tones. Contrary to its reputation, ochre is striking on its own and a natural mixer with most colors but pastels.

Ochre with Black: A fashionable and fail-safe way to wear ochre is to mix it with black. Shown in casual clothes in figures 1–4, this color mix could also work in luxury fabrics for evening dress. Choose simple, easy styles that convey the sharp modernity of this color combination.

Ochre with Black, Brights, Neutrals, and Jewel Tones: In figures 1–4, red, royal, and magenta soften the sharpness of the ochre-and-black combination. In figures 5, 7, and 8, ochre is combined with a variety of colors that are all regulars in the autumn color palette. The ochre is essential in ensuring that of these unlikely colors work together. In figure 6, ochre is combined with turquoise and purple. This combination may seem odd, but ochre gives these brights an autumn personality.

75

Malachite

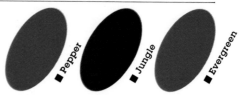

3 Variations of Malachite

The deep-jewel beauty of malachite merits special consideration. A rather obscure color, malachite has a surprising range and looks good with almost every skin tone. Malachite is traditionally used in a limited way, as a part of red and beige plaids or as a velvet color. In fact, the color-mixing possibilities are much greater and are explored in the next few pages.

Mixing Malachite with Basic Color Groups

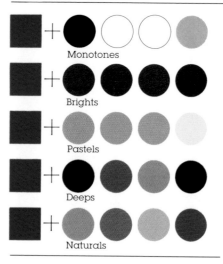

Monotones

Brights

Pastels

Deeps

Naturals

Malachite mixes well with all the basic monotones, particularly black. It can be used with pastels in much the same way as navy blue with this difficult color range. Neutrals accept malachite readily; use an accent color to prevent the green from overwhelming the beige.

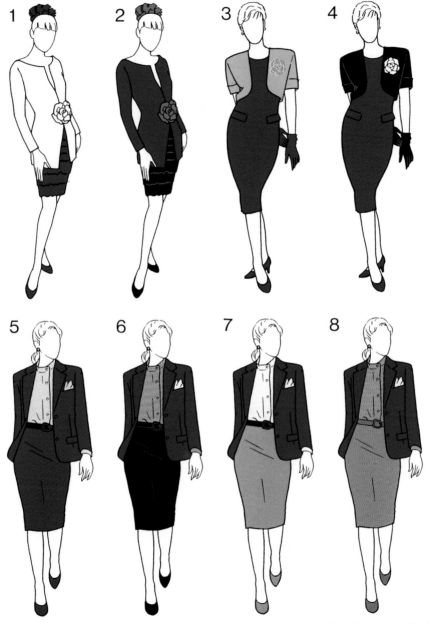

In the first four figures, where malachite is combined with monotones for evening dress, the black-malachite outfits (figures 2 and 4) are clearly the winners. The balance between malachite's dramatic dominance and black's coordinating accent keeps the color unusual and avoids harshness.

Figures 5–8 show malachite as a practical color that melds into a conservative office environment. None of these last four figures make particularly exciting fashion statements, but they do provide practical information.

Malachite

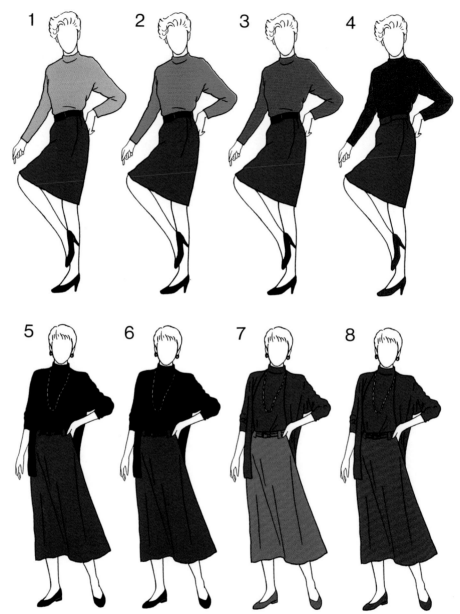

In figures 1–4, a malachite skirt is combined with a bright-colored sweater. Malachite is definitely an autumn color, and until recently, this kind of coordination would have been avoided, but a desire to wear brights all year round has expanded our ideas on how colors can be combined. In figures 5–8, malachite is used in a beautifully traditional way with claret, plum, olive, and brown—all members of the Fall color palette. In each example, this soft sophistication looks completely natural.

In figures 1–4, a bright element in varying amounts is offered in each of the outfits, making the coordination more complex. Neutrals soften the combinations, and white or black is brought in to provide contrast without adding another color. Although unlikely, these four combinations offer some ideas on how to exercise your coordination skills. In figures 5–8, multiple colors are again used, but they coordinate in a natural, less intellectual way. Neutrals and rich spice colors create an exotic color palette, known as "summer darks," but can be worn year round.

79

Navy

3 Variations of Navy

While navy blue is probably not your favorite color, it has an enduring character and a reputation for reliability and good taste. It appears throughout our lives, from school uniforms to corporate dress. Unfortunately, institutional uses of navy fail to explore its many attributes and affinities. Navy's personality expands and is reinvented as it is mixed, matched, and played against other colors.

Mixing Navy with Basic Color Groups

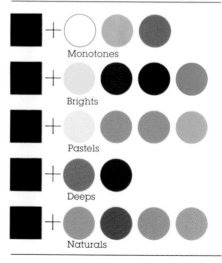

Navy is most often worn in a conservative way with monotones, particularly with grey or white in place of black. It mixes well with all brights and is good with pastels and naturals when the combinations are handled with some sensitivity.

Navy with White: Navy and white always signal the beginning of the Spring season and a new year. In figures 1 and 2, the blazer and skirt are fabricated in what might be a lightweight wool gabardine. Figures 3 and 4 introduce a more casual look; the navy and white stripes suggest a nautical styling traditionally used for these colors. In figures 6–8, the full potential of mix and match with navy and white is shown, playing the properness of the color against the softness of the styling.

Navy

Navy with Pastels and Soft Brights: Navy blue and pastel mixtures often recall memories of Easters pasl. Figures 1–4 have a sporty look—navy linen walking shorts with a cotton knit top in navy and white stripes or a fresh, clean solid color. The simply styled candy-colored jackets balance the deep color of the shorts. The easygoing college look in figures 5–8, where unrelated colors play against one another, shows that navy can work as well in jackets and sweaters as in pants and skirts.

82

Navy with Vivid Brights: The skirt in figures 1–4 is probably fabricated in a gauzy cotton, creating an indigo or ethnic image for hot Summer days. The deep, inky blue and hot brights are reminiscent of Mexico or Central America. The brightly colored sashes perfectly accentuate the festive moods of these combinations. Graphic styling brings a cool, precise look to the navy and bright mixes in figures 5–8.

Navy as a Professional Basic: Navy, which may already be the anchor for your professional wardrobe, is not as severe as black and projects a stable, corporate image appreciated in most offices. The navy blazer and skirt in figures 1–4 are mixed with such unobtrusive neutrals as beige, grey, and brown. Figures 5–8 have a softer look, and their character would be determined by the fabrics used. For example, a cashmere sweater with a silk shirt and soft wool skirt would create a relaxed, elegant image.

In figures 1–4, navy appears in a spectrum of browns. When contrasted with spicy browns, navy takes on a depth and range more like the traditional indigo blues of India and Japan. In figures 5–8, navy is shown in traditional combinations. The beige-and-navy plaid skirt (figure 5) is reliable. Navy with white and grey (figure 6) is more conservative but always acceptable. Navy combined with light brown and claret (figure 7) might best be described as intellectual. Red, white, and blue (figure 8) is ever-popular.

Plum

■ Raisin   ■ Damson

2 Variations of Plum

This dusky, mysterious color calls up visions of plush silk velvet and heavy silk satins. Luxurious plum is often overlooked because of the overriding popularity of the lighter, more versatile claret and purple. But plum has a provocative personality and can be many things, depending on the colors it's paired with. It works best as a Fall color but can be interesting in Summer linen or silk.

Mixing Plum with Basic Color Groups

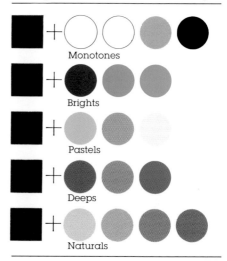

Monotones

Brights

Pastels

Deeps

Naturals

Monotones bring out the cool, dark side of plum's personality. When mixed with soft pastels and beiges, plum appears to be a deep dusky red. Combined with spice colors, plum becomes a warm reddish brown. Neutrals make plum appear to be almost black.

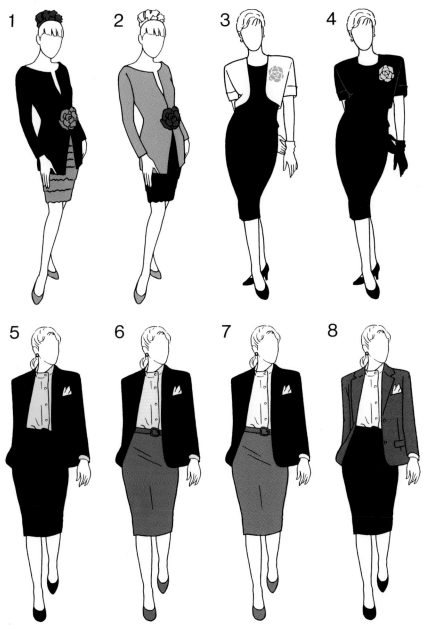

To ensure the correct color effect, it is important to select the right material to carry the plum. Figures 1–4 are very dressy, even though plum is used with monotones. Plum is most effective when it is put into luxury fabrics, such as velvet, taffeta, and silk faille. In figures 5–8, plum is shown as a color option for career dressing. Mixed with neutrals and soft pastels, plum offers an interesting alternative to the standard office colors of grey, beige, navy, and black.

Plum

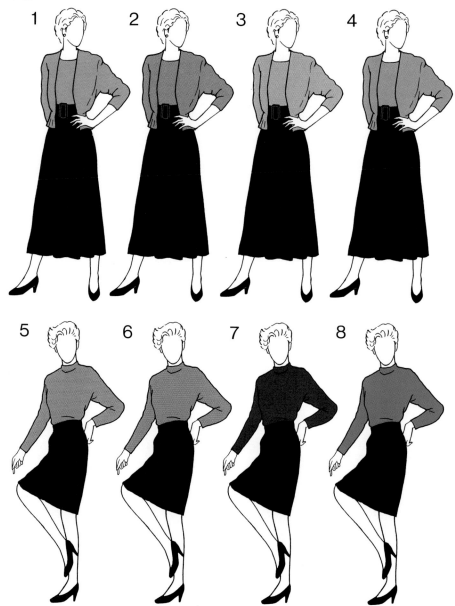

In figures 1–4, plum dresses down with a series of skirts and tops in neutrals and dusty pastels. Plum warms the grey and tan in figures 1 and 2 and encourages a soft sweetness from the pink and blue in figures 3 and 4. In figures 5 and 8, a variety of brights are paired with plum. Used in this pedestrian way, plum becomes just another dark color used to support the vibrant gold, pink, red, and green. The intensity of these colors squanders the depth and richness of plum.

The combinations in figures 1–4 take advantage of rather unusual colors, such as olive, curry, and warm carmel brown. The pale blouses in peach, beige, and tan that pull this look together. The combinations in figures 5–8 attain a highly individualized look. The soft pastel jackets accented by

beige and white in figures 5 and 6 leave the plum looking dark, but the combination would work if the pastels were a bit deeper. Figure 7 is also a bit off, but the olive, curry, and plum mix in figure 8 would work gloriously well in fine linen.

Beige

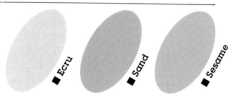

3 Variations of Beige

Ecru Sand Sesame

The word beige comes from the French and originally described wool in its natural unbleached state. The first beige was most likely a rough, earthy version with the imperfections of nature, but it has since come to identify a refined creamy color. Beige, like black, is a year-round classic whose personality depends on the composition and weave of the material that carries it.

Mixing Beige with Basic Color Groups

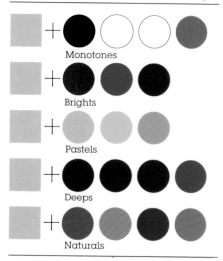

Monotones

Brights

Pastels

Deeps

Naturals

Beige, the anchor of the natural family, has endless versions—some with a touch of blue and others warmed with red—but each operates within the rigid confines of the color's neutrality. It wears well with other color groups except vivacious brights, which overwhelm it.

In figures 1-8, various combinations of beige and black are shown. Beige and black are appropriate in any season, in any fabrication—from the wool coating weight shown in figures 3 and 4 to the lightweight knits in figure 6. Beige and black can also work for relaxed, casual looks, such as the soft jacket and walking shorts in figure 8. Add white to freshen the combination or a touch of vivid color, such as the fiery scarf in figure 3.

Beige

Figures 1-8 mix beige with dusty pastels and other natural colors. The use of black and white as accent colors provides an edge to various combinations and ensures that the neutrals will never look washed out. Beige warms up with the peach and

aqua jackets in figures 3 and 4, as it does when mixed with browns in figures 5–8. These natural colors make beige look particularly good, and they can be worn easily by almost everyone.

Figures 1-8 combine beige with naturals and black. These colors suggest a warm, wooly Autumn mood, but try these combinations in lightweight linen for Spring and Summer. These natural "pebble" colors have been popular for several years, making them good candidates for serious investment dressing. In figures 5–8, beige is color-blocked with claret, malachite, terra cotta, and olive, each combination a well-balanced mix of light and dark.

Taupe

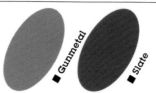

Gunmetal   Slate

2 Variations of Taupe

Taupe is a secondary color with an inconspicuous but tasteful character that makes it an alternative to charcoal and beige. Once considered an Autumn color, taupe now appears regularly as a Spring color in silk and linen. Taupe's soft brownish cast distinguishes it as a natural color that can be very beautiful when combined with other colors that accentuate its subtlety.

Mixing Taupe with Basic Color Groups

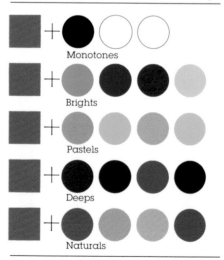

Monotones

Brights

Pastels

Deeps

Naturals

Taupe can be a lifeless neutral on its own but comes alive if mixed with monotones or other neutrals. The natural warmth of taupe is accentuated by pastels and pale naturals. Vivid brights will leech the life from taupe, but deep dark brights work if used sparingly.

Figures 1–4 combine taupe with black, white, navy, and beige to create a conservative corporate look. In figures 5–7, taupe is shown with monotones and neutrals, but the silhouette is sporty rather than professional. In figure 8, taupe blends with the delicate peach top and decidedly doesn't with the teal green shorts. The combination is unlikely and less successful than the other three figures in this series.

Taupe

Pastels are notoriously difficult to coordinate in a sophisticated way, but taupe is an exceptional vehicle for bringing out the best in this color range. In figures 1–4, the soft brown beauty of taupe transforms pink, blue, and peach from saccharine pastels to dusty pales. White and black sharpen the combinations, but even without a monotone edge, the color combination is beautiful. The mood changes radically in figures 5–8, where taupe is used as a neutral to support the vivid intensity of the brights.

In figures 1–4, taupe is combined with other naturals. This series suggests conventional and easy-to-understand ways to wear taupe. Except in figure 4, taupe is paired here with a warmer natural. Figures 5–8 suggest unusual color combinations with less-than-successful results. Strong colors in figures 5 and 7 rob taupe of its vitality. Only the brown ensemble in figure 8 that relies on black as an accent is attractive in a professional way.

Brown

2 Variations of Brown

Brown is an easy color to take for granted. It is regarded as a dull but reliable basic that never offends. Unfortunately, it has been treated this way for so long that it finally has become offensive. Once an everpresent standard like navy, brown is now an endangered species, overshadowed by turquoise, purple, copper, and khaki. Brown is a bit dreary, but it has innumerable attributes.

Mixing Brown with Basic Color Groups

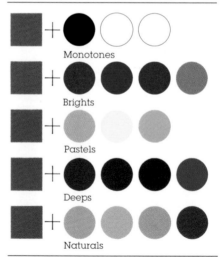

Brown is traditionally worn on its own or mixed with other naturals. Apart from that, brown has broad mixing potential. It is sophisticated with monotones, interesting with pastels, new and fashion-forward with brights, and elegant with jewel tones.

Brown as a Basic: In the first four figures, brown is coordinated in a very traditional way. Figures 5–8 offer several ways to expand this look into something more adventurous. A splash of bright red in figures 5 and 7 sparks an otherwise heavy black-brown combination. The white blouse in figure 6 keeps the look fresh and professional. In figure 8, brown predominates, with black as an accent. The modern graphic quality of this combination is echoed by the grid pattern on the skirt.

Brown

Brown with Brights: Figures 1–4 combine brown with spicy brights. Black is used as an accent to keep the look succinct and modern. For simplicity's sake, the combination has been carefully limited to the two colors and black. The color palette in figures 5–8 is also restricted. The brightly colored pullovers keep the high color near the face, with brown relegated to the pants.

Brown with Naturals, Pastels, and Grey:
Again, black is the perfect accent in the soft, sophisticated look in figures 1–4. Pink with brown in figure 1 is an unusual but flattering mix. The same soft dusty feeling is achieved when brown is mixed with grey in figure 2 and mauve in figure 3. In figure 4, family colors are paired for a staid but attractive combination. The mood changes with figures 5–8, where brown is mixed with two brights. The color mixing here is relatively complex and requires an artful balancing between brights and naturals.

Carmel Brown

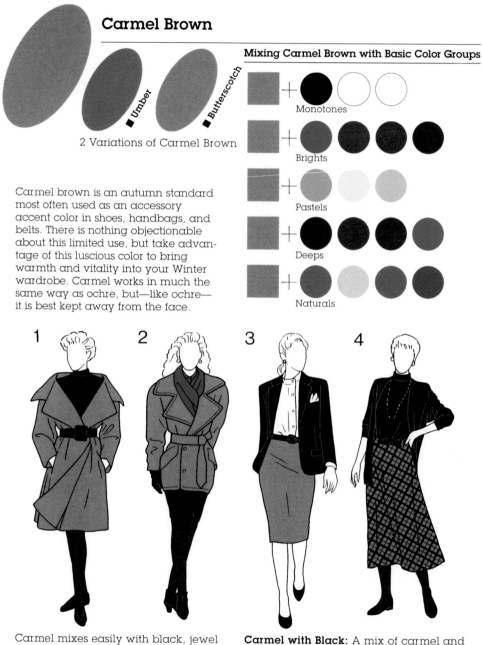

2 Variations of Carmel Brown

■ Umber   ■ Butterscotch

Mixing Carmel Brown with Basic Color Groups

Monotones

Brights

Pastels

Deeps

Naturals

Carmel brown is an autumn standard most often used as an accessory accent color in shoes, handbags, and belts. There is nothing objectionable about this limited use, but take advantage of this luscious color to bring warmth and vitality into your Winter wardrobe. Carmel works in much the same way as ochre, but—like ochre—it is best kept away from the face.

Carmel mixes easily with black, jewel brights, and natural colors. It overwhelms beiges and pastels, so avoid mixing it with pale colors. Instead, match carmel with strong, dramatic colors and enjoy the range of possibilities you have created for Winter.

Carmel with Black: A mix of carmel and black offers instant sophistication and ease. The royal blue scarf in figure 2 and the white blouse in figure 3 soften the potentially harsh look and keep carmel away from the face.

Carmel Brown with Naturals and Brights:
The naturals in figures 1–3 are traditionally mixed with carmel and go together without any problem. The brights and jewel colors in figures 4–8 make more interesting combinations and offer suggestions on expanding your wardrobe in ways that you had probably never considered. Note that the carmel is usually shown as a pant or skirt, with the brighter color on top. Black accents are used as belts, bags, and scarves.

Khaki

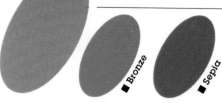

2 Variations of Khaki

Mixing Khaki with Basic Color Groups

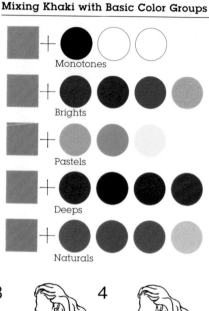

Monotones

Brights

Pastels

Deeps

Naturals

Khaki, a popular summer neutral originally used exclusively in fashionable menswear, acquired a universal appeal in the seventies, when women's sportswear began to grow in importance. Khaki's easy, unobtrusive personality mixes easily with most other color families. It is an anchor that other colors (apart from the difficult pastel group) can work off of.

Avoid wearing khaki on its own—it is draining next to the face and can look severe and institutional. With monotones, on the other hand, khaki mixes beautifully. It is fresh and clean when combined with white, and cool and sophisticated when mixed with black.

Figures 1–4 use red as an accent: the red belt in figure 1 sparks the khaki-black combination; in figures 2–4, red is used as a cotton knit top, keeping the khaki and the black away from the face.

Figures 1 and 2 show khaki in its most famous form—the casual khaki pant—tastefully paired with a simple crew-neck sweater in traditional burgundy and navy blue. These deep colors enhance the rich golden khaki and are reliable color mates.

In figures 3 and 4, khaki is adventurously mixed with vivid jewel brights, In figures 5–8, khaki is used as a ground color for several graphic prints. The reddish brown tones in figures 5 and 7 are good colors with khaki.

Olive

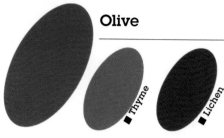

2 Variations of Olive

Mixing Olive with Basic Color Groups

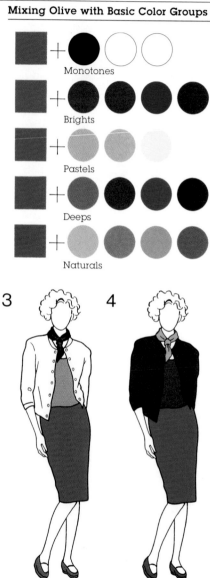

+ Monotones

+ Brights

+ Pastels

+ Deeps

+ Naturals

Worn alone, olive is a drab, severe color that invariably invites unflattering comparisons to military uniforms. Olive's strength is that it enhances other colors and mixes well with a variety of color families, from naturals to brights. A standard issue for Fall, olive is now equally popular for Spring and Summer, appearing on silk, cotton, and rayon in exotic tropical prints.

Olive is least successful with monotones. When mixed with white and black, olive is usually treated like charcoal. The result is uninspired at best and dreary at worst. Olive works best with strong colors, as in figure 1. The severity of the olive-black combination in figure 2 is relieved with a warm, natural color. The white sweater and the olive skirt in figure 3 look mismatched. The fourth figure is the most successful, because the olive skirt is mixed with wine, an elegant purple, and accented with a gold scarf.

106

Olive, like charcoal, is one of the few colors that works in a sophisticated way with pastels. In figures 1 and 2, sporty jackets in pink and soft rose linen or light wool are casually worn over olive walking shorts. In figures 3 and 4, olive in the flared skirt is combined with the deep jewel colors of wine and purple. In figure 6, the bright red brings up the green in the olive. The rich brights in figures 7 and 8 also enliven the deep green of the color and show olive at its best.

Coordinating Coats and Scarves
Black Coats

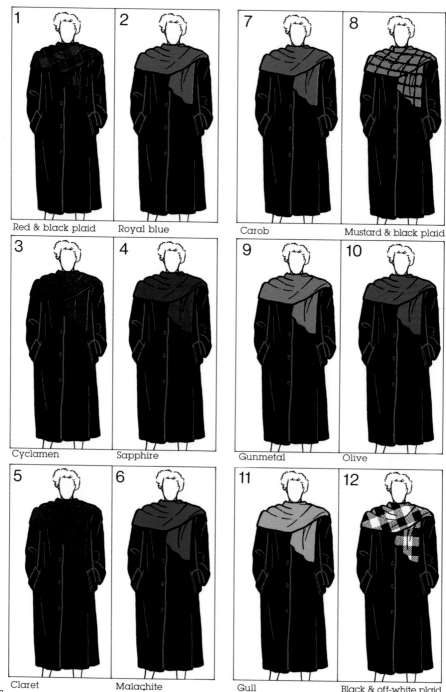

1. Red & black plaid
2. Royal blue
3. Cyclamen
4. Sapphire
5. Claret
6. Malachite
7. Carob
8. Mustard & black plaid
9. Gunmetal
10. Olive
11. Gull
12. Black & off-white plaid

Coordinating Coats and Scarves
Dark Blue Coats

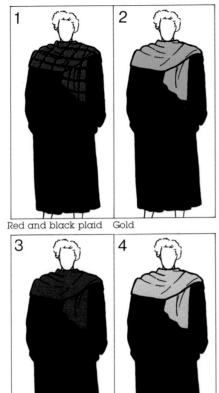

1 — Red and black plaid   2 — Gold

3 — Elderberry   4 — Powder pink

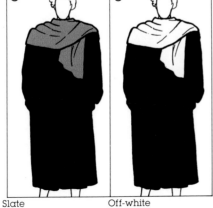

5 — Slate   6 — Off-white

Grey Coats

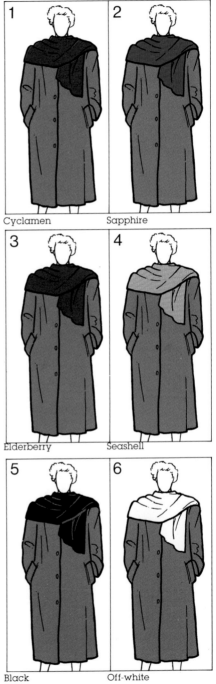

1 — Cyclamen   2 — Sapphire

3 — Elderberry   4 — Seashell

5 — Black   6 — Off-white

109

Coordinating Coats and Scarves

Khaki Brown Coats

Taupe Coats

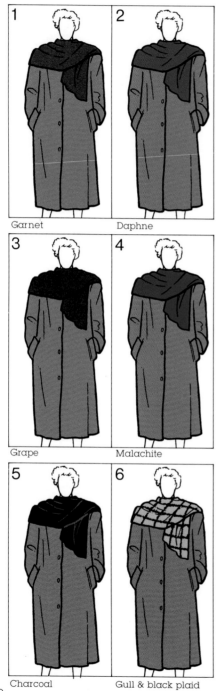

Khaki Brown Coats:
1. Garnet
2. Daphne
3. Grape
4. Malachite
5. Charcoal
6. Gull & black plaid

Taupe Coats:
1. Garnet
2. Sapphire
3. Bisque
4. Evergreen
5. Charcoal
6. Camel & charcoal plaid

Coordinating Coats and Scarves
Olive Coats

1 Red & black plaid
2 Magenta
3 Heliotrope
4 Gold & black plaid
5 Umber
6 Charcoal

Red Coats

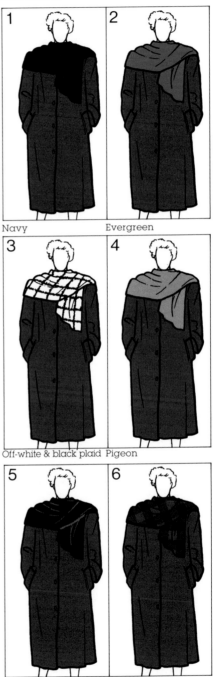

1 Navy
2 Evergreen
3 Off-white & black plaid
4 Pigeon
5 Charcoal
6 Garnet & black plaid

111

The Color Circle

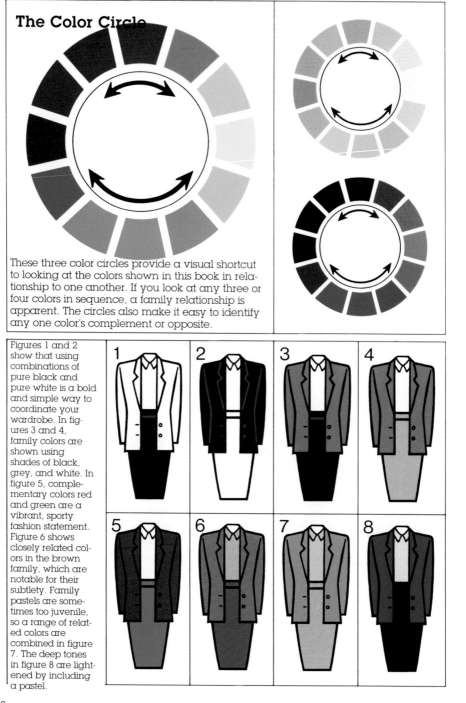

These three color circles provide a visual shortcut to looking at the colors shown in this book in relationship to one another. If you look at any three or four colors in sequence, a family relationship is apparent. The circles also make it easy to identify any one color's complement or opposite.

Figures 1 and 2 show that using combinations of pure black and pure white is a bold and simple way to coordinate your wardrobe. In figures 3 and 4, family colors are shown using shades of black, grey, and white. In figure 5, complementary colors red and green are a vibrant, sporty fashion statement. Figure 6 shows closely related colors in the brown family, which are notable for their subtlety. Family pastels are sometimes too juvenile, so a range of related colors are combined in figure 7. The deep tones in figure 8 are lightened by including a pastel.

Silhouettes

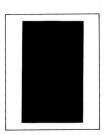

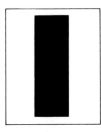

1. Straight Line: A long rectangular silhouette that drops straight off the shoulder and finishes at the hem.

2. Box Line: A square or shallow rectangular shape that drops from a broad shoulder line and finishes at the hem.

3. Tapered Line: The silhouette drops from an exaggerated shoulder and oversized blouse that tapers to a narrow skirt at the hem.

4. Trapeze Line: A silhouette that drops from narrow shoulders, grazes the bust, moves away from the waist, and flares at the hem.

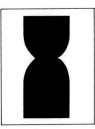

5. Fit and Flared Line: A silhouette that tapers from an exaggerated shoulder to a narrow waist and then flares out once again to the hem.

6. Wine Glass Line: A silhouette with a voluminous top and fitted from the waist to the hem.

7. Bell Line: A silhouette that has a fitted torso and a hip-to-hem curvature that is shaped like a bell.

8. Hour Glass Line: A silhouette with a full bust, pinched waist, and full curving hip that follows a straight line to the hem.

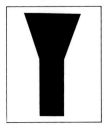

9. Champagne Glass Line: A silhouette with an acute shoulder line that tapers from the waist to the hem.

10. Spinning Top Line: A silhouette with a straight, slender bodice, flaring at the hip and tapering at the hem.

11. Mermaid Line: Also known as the trumpet line. A silhouette with a long, fitted torso, flaring from mid-thigh to hem.

12. Balloon Line: A silhouette that drops from the shoulder to a cinched hem below the knee.

Collars

1. Shirt Collar: A tailored, turned-down collar appropriate both for men's and women's shirts. This basic collar fits easily against the neck.

2. Button-Down Collar: The basic shirt style, with the collar points affixed to the body of the shirt with small buttons.

3. Round Collar: Same as the basic shirt collar, but with rounded ends in the front.

4. Polo Collar: A knitted collar on a casual sports shirt with a three-button placket opening.

5. Convertible Collar: A rolled collar that can be worn open—showing a small lapel—or closed—by buttoning the collar at the neck.

6. Notched Convertible Collar: Can be worn open or closed and is distinguished by its wide-angled spread in the front.

7. Spread Collar: Styled after a man's shirt, this collar is set on a narrow band and has widely spaced collar points.

8. Horizontal Collar: Similar to the spread collar, but the front points lie on a 180-degree angle.

9. Italian Collar: This collar is made in one piece by cutting, facing, and turning the center front of the blouse over.

10. Notched Collar: A tailored style that has a notch cut away where the lapel and collar join.

11. Tailored Collar: This style was once considered the only appropriate choice for any woman wearing a tailored suit.

12. Ulster Collar: A version of the notched collar, primarily used for coats and suits.

13. Stand-Up Collar: Also known as a banded collar. A straight piece that extends up the neck and is attached to the body of the shirt.

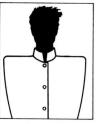

14. Military Collar: This one is borrowed from the military dress uniform and is notched in the center front.

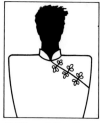

15. Chinese Collar: Also known as a Mandarin collar, this banded collar extends up the neck and tapers to center front without actually meeting.

16. Stand-Off Collar: Usually a roll-away collar that stands away from the neck. This style is often fabricated in a knit.

114

17. Bermuda Collar: Lying flat on the garment, this rounded collar's pointed ends finish in right-angled corners.

18. Spread Collar: This basic style follows a curve along the neckline and angles into two broadly spaced points in the front.

19. Peter Pan Collar: A small, flat collar with rounded front ends. Often used for children's clothes.

20. Puritan Collar: This collar extends to the shoulder seams at the sides and ends in two long points at the center front.

21. Sailor Collar: A large collar inspired by the Navy "middy" blouse, featuring a piece that hangs down the back and tapers to a V in the front.

22. Petal Collar: This feminine style is composed of overlapping sections that resemble the petals of a flower.

23. Shawl Collar: A collar without lapels; that is, cut in one piece and folded over to follow the front opening of the garment.

24. Stand-Away Collar: This collar stands away from the neck and rolls over, creating a widely spaced spread between the collar points.

25. Cross Muffler Collar: A type of shawl collar that crosses at the bottom of the shawl. A style favored for knitted fabrics.

26. Sideways Collar: The front of this collar follows the soft, deep V of the neckline and finishes off center at either the right or left.

27. Rolled Scoop Collar: This collar stands away from the neck and follows a scooped-out line.

28. Pipe Collar: This collar extends up from the shoulder and finishes just under the chin. Usually used on coats.

29. Ascot Collar: The bands are attached at the back of the neck, brought around to the front, and looped with one band falling down over the other.

30. Bow Collar: To achieve this feminine collar, an extended band is attached to the neckline and then tied in a bow in the front.

31. Cascading Collar: An asymmetrical ruffle is cut from a circular piece and attached to the neckline of the blouse.

32. Ruffled Collar: This romantic collar is cut on the cross-grain, or bias, and attached to a scooped-out neckline to create a petal-like frame.

Necklines

1. Jewel: A simple, round, unembellished neckline that serves as a backdrop for a necklace or other jewelry.

2. Crew: A rounded neckline finished with knit ribbing. This style originated on crew racing shirts.

3. Bateau: This neckline is split from shoulder to shoulder, while remaining high against the neck in both the front and the back.

4. Off the Shoulder: Low in front and back, the part of the neckline extending around the upper part of the arm is often elasticized or knit to permit easy movement.

5. V: A V-shape angled in from the shoulder to the center front.

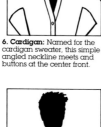

6. Cardigan: Named for the cardigan sweater, this simple angled neckline meets and buttons at the center front.

7. Surplice: A V-shape is created in the front when one side of a wrap-around blouse crosses over and fastens on the opposite side.

8. Halter: A sleeveless bodice secured by a band around the neck.

9. Square: Also known as the "Dutch neckline," this style is squared in front and sometimes in back as well.

10. Sweetheart: The sides of this low-cut neckline slant toward the front, curving together in a heart shape.

11. Choker: High and close to the neck, this neckline usually fastens in the back.

12. Funnel: This neckline resembles an inverted funnel, because it is made with the shoulder seams slanting up toward the neck.

13. Turtle: A high, close-fitting neckline that rolls over the top once (and sometimes two or three times if made from knitted fabric).

14. Camisole: A feminine neckline cut low, straight across the bust, and secured with straps over the shoulders.

15. Strapless: Bare in front and in back, the bodice is often secured with bones, stays, or darts, because—as its name implies—there are no straps or sleeves to hold it up.

16. One Shoulder: Also known as the "swing neck." This neckline runs at an oblique line from one shoulder to the other, leaving the remaining shoulder bare.

1. Set In: A general term used to describe any sleeve set into a natural armhole.

2. Pagoda: The shape of this sleeve, which resembles the roof of a pagoda, is distinguished by its funnel-shaped outer sleeve, which flares at the wrist.

3. Petal: This short, curved sleeve overlaps in the front, creating a petal-like effect.

4. Sleeveless: Literally, no sleeve. Traditionally, the armhole is round and finished with bias binding or a facing.

5. Dolman: A seamless sleeve, like a kimono sleeve, with the underarm beginning well below the natural armhole and finishing tightly at the wrist.

6. Batwing: This dramatic sleeve comes out of a deep armhole and is caught at the wrist. It takes its name from the cape-like effect created in the back.

7. Wedge: An angled, set-in sleeve that creates a modified dolman.

8. Drop Shoulder: The seam is set off the natural shoulder, allowing the garment a natural, easygoing look.

9. Puff: This ultra-sweet style is gathered at both the armhole and the cuff, a construction creating the dramatic effect that inspires its name.

10. Balloon: A large, mid-length puffed sleeve that is set into the armhole.

11. Peasant: This folk-inspired style is usually long and full with gathering at the armhole and the wrist.

12. Leg of Mutton: This sleeve is full at the cap and then gathered or pleated into the armhole and finished tightly at the wrist.

13. Raglan: A set-in sleeve that angles from the front underarm inward toward the neckline.

14. Modified Raglan: The underarm seam of this sleeve runs toward the center front but only as far as the shoulder.

15. French: A seamless sleeve that is an extension of the front and back of the garment. The slope of the shoulder creates the shape of the sleeve.

16. Cap: A small, neat sleeve that "caps" the natural shoulder.

Glossary

Abstract: In fashion, usually referring to a print or an unusual use of line.

Accent color: A color used in small amounts (often in such accessories as shoes, a belt, or a scarf) to enhance other colors in the outfit.

Acetate: A synthetic fabric made from cellulose acetate and primarily used for the linings of sportswear and coats. This lightweight, slippery fabric is an economical substitute for silk.

Achromatic color: Black or white; that which has no color; a non-color.

Acrylic: A man-made fiber made from resins. Acrylics are easy to care for, mildew-proof, crease-resistant, and hold a pleat permanently.

Active sportswear: Category of clothing (originally called "sports suits") designed to be worn for specific active sports, such as tennis and bicycling.

Advancing color: A color that appears to come forward in a pattern; red, yellow, and yellow-green are examples.

American style: In contrast to European or Japanese style; typically, this style is sporty, preppy, casual, and easygoing.

Animal print: A cloth pattern representing the skin of an exotic animal, such as a zebra or a leopard.

Apparel: Synonymous with clothes, dress, garment, attire, garb; basically any type of clothing worn by men, women, and children.

Apparel industry: The enterprise of manufacturing textiles, clothing, and accessories.

Appliqué: A decorative treatment in which a cut-out of one fabric is embroidered or stitched onto a second fabric.

Art deco: The decorative and fine arts movement that began in France and England in the early twenties. Characterized by stylish, geometric patterns; typical colors used are gold, silver, and black.

Art nouveau: Decorative and fine art originating in France, Germany, Belgium, and Austria in the late 19th century. Linear and curvilinear designs appearing in interior decoration and architecture, including the Paris subway stations.

Art to wear: Hand-crafted clothing or accessories distinguished for their artistry, with wearability and practicality being secondary considerations. These "one of a kind" pieces are never mass-manufactured and are made by craftspersons known for their technique (weaving, appliqué, etc.).

Asymmetry: Without symmetry; unbalanced; used to create movement by breaking the symmetry.

Avant-garde: New and ahead of the time; forward-thinking and often startling; the elixir of fashion.

Baby blue: A pale shade of blue that is traditionally worn by baby boys.

Baby pink: A pastel or light shade of pink traditionally worn by baby girls.

Basic color: In determining color schemes, one of the major colors to choose from—often black, beige, white, or grey.

Beachwear: Apparel or accessories specifically designed to be worn by the pool or at the beach,

Black tie: Men's semi-formal dress. As opposed to "white-tie," which is formal, or "casual," which is informal.

Blazer: A single-breasted sport jacket originally worn by men but later translated into women's fashion, where it has become a broadly interpreted sportswear basic.

Blouson: A women's jacket or shirt that blouses and is drawn in at the waist or slightly below the waist.

Bodice: The upper part or torso of a dress, blouse, or jump suit.

Body conscious: A silhouette or garment that accentuates the body shape.

Body suit: A one-piece fitted garment (often called a "cat suit") usually made of a stretchy synthetic or knitted fabric that accentuates the figure. The body suit can be worn on its own or in combination with other garments.

Border print: A design that runs along a hem or cuff.

Bright color: Clear, clean saturated color—usually red, orange, yellow, blue, or green; can also include pink, turquoise, and purple.

Career dressing: A dress code for the professional woman. Usually a conservative look styled to fit into what was originally "a man's world." The basic look includes a tailored blazer, a straight skirt, and a detailed blouse.

Cashmere: A luxury fabric made from the hair of the cashmere goat, which is found in Kashmir, India, Tibet, and China. The wool is obtained by combing, not clipping, the goat. The resulting woven fabric is known for its warmth, softness, and high price.

Casual wear: Informal, everyday clothing, typical of the American lifestyle.

CFDA: The Council of Fashion Designers of America—a non-profit organization of America's foremost designers founded in 1962. Norman Norell was the first president. Membership is by invitation only.

Chanel suit: A woman's suit designed by the French designer Gabrielle "Coco" Chanel; simple skirt and short, collarless jacket.

Chic: Sophisticated or stylish.

Chinois: Chinese style.

City wear: Street clothing with a sophisticated fashion image.

Classic: Traditional, timeless. Describing styles that have been popular for a long time. Fashion is an ongoing cycle of new trendy and classic styles.

Collection: A preseason showing of a designer's line; usually held twice a year for Spring/Summer and Fall/Winter fashions.

Color blocking: Placing predetermined amounts of color side by side within a single garment to make a visual color statement. In fine art, Mondrian was the greatest of all color blockers.

Color coordinating: Planning an outfit by considering the relationships of the colors to be worn.

Conservative: Traditional; staying away from fashion trends and keeping to traditional styles.

Contemporary: Current; having the look of today; the now look.

Cool color: A color with a blue undertone and suggesting serenity. Cool colors include blue, green, and purple.

Corduroy: Derived from the French term "corde du roi," meaning cloth of the French royalty; like denim, widely used by people of all ages.

Cosmetic color: A color relating to makeup for the face; for example, peach, pink, beige.

Costume: Stylized and coordinated clothes or dress based on a theme or story.

Costume jewelry: Originally, inexpensive jewelry used in a play; today, accessories.

Couture: A French word describing original fashion design produced by hand in such fashion houses as Dior, Chanel, and Ungaro. The couture collections are shown twice a year in Paris, Milan, and London and are the inspiration for the less-expensive ready-to-wear collections that follow.

Cross-dyed: A textile term that identifies fabrics woven of two or more fibers spun from different kinds of materials but dyed together. Because of their different compositions, the fibers accept dye differently. This variation shows up in the weave, creating interesting textual effects.

Culottes: Originally, short pants worn by men in late 17th- and early 18th-century France; today, a divided skirt (wide-legged trousers) for contemporary fashion.

Damask: Originally, a luxurious textile from Damascus. Particularly suited to blouse and jacket fabrics, damask is a kind of jacquard or double weave that makes its design through the contrast of shiny and matte finishes.

Dandy: A man who is unusually attentive to the fashion and coordination of his clothing.

Décolléte: Describing a neckline that is cut very low, exposing the shoulders, neck, back, and upper part of the bosom.

Demonde: Out of fashion or passe.

Denim: A casual, sturdy woven twill originally used as tenting fabric. In 1849 Levi Strauss began to use it to make pants for miners in San Francisco. Although denim is synonymous with blue, it can be dyed any color. The popularity of denim is universal and supports an enormous industry.

Designer: A creator of original fashion. Designers work in the various areas of the fashion industry, which includes both clothing and accessories. Some designers own their own businesses, and others are hired to develop collections for a label.

Designer label: Literally, a woven label sewn into the garment that identifies the designer. Or, the top tier of manufactured clothing, reflecting originality, quality, and price.

Divided skirt: See *Culottes*.

Double-breasted: Describing a garment (usually a jacket) with a front opening that laps over double and fastens with two rows of buttons. Originally, both sets of buttons were functional; today, one set is decorative.

Drape: The way a fabric falls or hangs on the body.

Earth colors: Colors that are found in nature and relate to the brown family—sienna, ochre, brown tones, and dark green. Natural plant dyes are often used to color natural fibers.

Electric color: A brilliant color.

Ensemble: An outfit with a look of unity and coordination; often one material is used for all pieces of the outfit.

Glossary

Epaulet: A decorative shoulder treatment borrowed from military jackets.

Ethnic: Native, traditional.

Fabric: A material, such as cloth, made from fibers by weaving, knitting, felting, etc.

Fashion coordinator: A specialist in the styling of fashionable clothes.

Fashion forecast: Usually a subscription service that predicts the upcoming fashion trends for color and silhouette. Designers and merchandisers use the forecast when designing their collections, with a mind to providing their potential customers with what they will want to buy at a given time and place.

Fashion-forward: At the forefront of a new fashion trend. Also called "advanced fashion." The opposite of classic or basic dressing.

Fashion trend: The direction in which fashion is moving at any given time; usually influenced by famous people or current events in the arts, politics, movies, and sports.

Fashion victims: Unfortunate beings who think only about being first in the latest look, with little thought given to how the fashion looks on them. These fashion groupies usually wear extreme, bizarre fashions.

Faux: False, imitation; used in conjunction with prints, jewelry, or furs. Something faux can be a fashion trend in itself—as in faux animal prints.

Fiber: Literally, "thread." Yarns are made from strands or filaments of fiber. The fiber can come from natural materials—such as cotton or wool—or from synthetic filaments—such as polyester and acetate.

Folkloric: Characteristic of ethnic styles.

Formal: Describing a dress code requiring evening dress for women, tuxedos for men.

Foulard: Also called "gun twill." A twill made of a lightweight silky material and decorated with a small printed design. Foulards are used for scarves, neckties, and dresses.

Foundation: An undergarment to smooth the figure; basic facial cosmetics.

Frock: Old-fashioned term for dress.

Gabardine: A sturdy twill weave that is most commonly woven in cotton or wool. A traditional sportswear fabric popularly used for skirts, pants, jackets, and coats.

Haberdashery look: An appearance evoked by combining several tailored men's wear prints and textures in one outfit. The jacket and shirt shapes also suggest a men's wear look.

Hand: The texture and weight of a fabric; more specifically, the quality of the weave.

Haute couture: Literally, "high sewing," referring to the original designs—usually custom-made by Saint Laurent or Ungaro—of the European fashion houses. Very expensive.

Hem: To finish off a garment by turning over the fabric and sewing it down so a clean edge remains.

Herringbone: A geometric pattern running in a continuous chevron, like the bones of a fish. This popular pattern is used in wovens, prints, knits, and fur designs.

High fashion: Haute couture before it becomes current fashion.

Houndstooth: Painted check pattern woven into fabric for men's and women's fashion.

Imitation: A fake or copy, usually of furs or jewelry. Cheaper than the real thing, fake accessories and furs have been very popular in recent seasons.

Impact color: Pure color used to create a shocking effect; for example, a bright red fire engine.

Indigo: A natural deep-blue dye made from the indigo plant.

Inner wear: A fashion industry term used to describe underwear or lingerie.

Iridescent: Having or showing an interplay of rainbow-like colors. A look achieved by weaving together two kinds of fibers, such as rayon and polyester.

Ivy League: A popular look for men in the fifties that originated on such campuses as Harvard, Princeton, and Yale; a forerunner to the preppie look; a style characterized by button-down collar shirts and pants with a small buckle in the back.

Jacquard: A design achieved by knitting on a special loom; invented by Frenchman Joseph Jacquard in 1801. Punch cards are used to separate and control the warp yarns.

Jeans: Originally, work clothes made of denim. In the sixties, denim jeans became big fashion, and the style spread worldwide.

Jewel tones: Deep hues of red, blue, green, and purple with the richness and intensity of fine gems.

Jump suit: A one-piece garment with pants; popular as casual fashion in the seventies and eighties.

Jungle print: A pattern depicting tropical plants, animals, or other elements of the tropics.

Junk jewelry: Imitation jewelry; fun accessories.

Jodhpurs: Indian word for riding breeches that are loose at the hip and tight from the knee to the ankle. Jodhpurs were once used exclusively for equestrian wear but are now used in fashion sportswear as a kind of trouser.

Khaki: A color name that means "earth" in Hindi and indicates a dark or greenish yellow; often, a military or safari color.

Kimono: The traditional dress of Japanese people. A straight robe that is tightly sashed at the waist with an *obi*. The sleeves are set in at right angles.

Knickers: Knickerbockers. In the late 19th century, men's short pants designed for bicycle riding; these often enjoy a fashion revival. In England, knickers are underpants.

Knockoffs: Inexpensive copies of high-priced designer fashion.

Label: Literally, the small woven label sewn into the garment that identifies the designer or manufacturer.

Lapel: The turned-back front section of a jacket, coat, blouse, or dress that joins to the collar.

Layered: Describing a fashion look in which layers of clothing are worn in noticeably different lengths.

Le dernier cri: In French, "the last word," the latest styles.

Length: A measurement to the lower edge of a garment. The hem of a coat, jacket, skirt, or dress. Standard lengths include mini, knee, calf, ballerina, ankle, and full.

Liberty prints: Small flower patterns from the Liberty of London Company in England.

Lingerie: Women's decorative underwear, such as a camisole, emphasizing femininity.

Look: A distinctive image with the potential of being a fashion direction. Looks often come from the movies, music, or news events. An example from the past is the flapper look; a current example is the Madonna look.

Loungewear: Casual clothes usually worn around the home and not on the street. Popular loungewear pieces include caftans and jump suits.

Lycra: Trademark of E.I. Du Pont de Nemours and Company for filament spandex fiber. Lycra is usually used as a blend with cotton or other fibers. Even a small amount of Lycra gives fabrics stretch and recovery. Originally, Lycra was used exclusively for swimwear and undergarments but is now popular for body-conscious sportswear and dresses.

Made-to-measure: Describing a garment that is cut and sewn based on an individual's measurement. No fittings are necessary. This type of work is done best in Hong Kong.

Maillot: A woman's one-piece bathing suit having a classic and simple style that is without embellishment and emphasizes the natural shape of the body.

Mannequin: A model whose job is to wear a designer's new collection in a fashion show. Also, the fashion statues that retail stores use to display current merchandise.

Man-tailored: Describing women's garments that are constructed and tailored like men's suits and coats, as opposed to the soft construction that typifies women's tailoring.

Marble print: A speckled pattern that imitates natural stone patterns; used in shoes, bags, and accessories.

Men's wear look: Women's clothing made from traditional men's wear fabrics. These are often man-tailored looks that mix plaids and stripes in unconventional ways.

Merchandising: The presentation of new products. All aspects of a product—including design, quality, and consumer demand—must be considered.

Midi: French term originally referring to a skirt length that came to the mid-calf of the leg. In the early seventies, this length became very popular, and the word was used to describe the mid-calf length of all garments.

Mini: French term originally referring to a skirt length that ends at mid-thigh. This length was popular in the sixties, and the word was used to describe any short garment.

Mismatched: Unexpected combinations such as a silk blouse with a leather jacket, lace worn with mannish pants, plaids with tweeds, and two different weaves in the same ensemble.

Mode: Fashion; originally, haute couture.

Modernism: Fashion in the twenties and thirties that emphasized function.

Monotone: A single color; a black or white color scheme.

Glossary

Muslin pattern: A garment made of an inexpensive fabric to verify the fit. Once adjustments are made, the muslin can be taken apart and used as a pattern for the actual garment.

Natural colors: Colors—soft in hue and image—relating to beige or grey. These colors are popular choices for Summer fashion. Grey, soft blue, pink, peach, off-white, and beige are the important natural colors.

Natural fibers: Cotton, silk, wool, and linen, all of which occur in nature. The opposite of fibers that are made from synthetics or chemicals.

Nautical: Silhouettes and motifs adapted for current fashion from naval uniforms. It is a crisp, fresh look often shown for early Spring wear in red, white, and blue. While most clothing with a nautical inspiration is sporty, the theme is sometimes carried into day and evening wear.

Neckline: The styling or contour of a garment at the neck and shoulders. The broad range of necklines includes V-neck and turtleneck.

Neoclassic: Designating modern styles that incorporate traditional design ideas.

Neutral colors: Non-colors; colors without hue and visible wavelength. Black, white, and grey are true neutrals. Adding black or white to a pure color lightens or darkens it, neutralizing the pure hue.

Nonwoven fabrics: Usually, synthetic fabrics constructed by interlocking or bonding fibers through thermal or chemical means.

Ombre: A color merge created by laying down light-to-dark gradations of a color; moving from pale pink to red, for example.

Oxford: Describing cloth that has a diagonal weave and is named for the town and university of Oxford, England. Originally, this cloth was used for the tennis wear of the university team.

Paisley: Printed with arabesque patterns. Originally from ancient India and Persia, paisley designs were popularized by 18th-century wool weavers in Paisley, Scotland. The paisley pattern has both an ethnic and an exotic quality.

Panache: Originally, a small feather plume; now, dash or style.

Pastel color: A pale, soft color made by adding white to a bright color; a color typical of Spring.

Patchwork: A folk design made from sewing small patches of cloth together; traditionally used for cushion and bed covers but now also used for accessories and embroidered clothes.

Peasant look: An appearance created from a romantic image of simplicity, usually with a full skirt and embroidered blouse.

Petite: A size range for women who are below average height but are in proportion to their height. This size range is usually numbered from 6 to 16.

Piece goods: Fabric sold by the yard, usually for home sewing. Also used in wholesale; designers and manufacturers buy a "piece"of goods, which is usually from 60 to 100 yards of one fabric on a roll.

Plaid: A generic term describing weaves of varying stripes of color running along both the warp and the weft. Even though plaids can be made up of any color in any right-angled configuration, the term is often used to describe the tartan patterns that the Scots use to designate different clans.

Polo shirt: Originally, a shirt worn for polo playing; now, fashionable sportswear, often with a small logo on the chest pocket.

Polyester: A synthetic fabric that is shrink-proof, moth-proof, and wrinkle-resistant. Polyester is often blended with natural fabrics to give these fabrics easy-care qualities.

Postmodern: Describing a trend that emphasizes decoration, as opposed to modernism's emphasis on function.

Preppie: Son of Ivy League; a collegiate look characterized by polo shirts, chinos, and navy blazers. Ralph Lauren is the sitting god to the preppies.

Prêt-à-porter: Ready to wear; can be popular styles or haute couture.

Primary colors: Red, blue, and yellow. All other colors are derived from these three colors.

Print: A design put onto fabric, usually with screen printing, rotary printing, or by hand, using two or more colors. Most countries have printed fabrics that reflect the specific culture.

Print-on-print: Having one pattern printed on a contrasting pattern—for example, flowers on stripes, wearing different patterns together.

Pullover: An outer layer, usually a sweater, without buttons.

Pure color: The clearest color value.

Glossary

Rayon: Generic term for fibers made from trees, cotton, and woody plants. Originally known as artificial silk because of its silky hand and highly lustrous appearance.

Ready-to-wear: Describing mass-produced apparel made in standard sizes. The opposite of couture. Known in France as "prêt-à-porter" and in England as "off-the-peg."

Receding color: A dark color or color value that appears smaller than it really is because it seems to reduce or minimize.

Reversible: Wearable with either side out.

Safari look: A style derived from clothing worn for hunting big game in Africa; a jacket with patch pockets and a belt, usually in khaki-colored cloth.

Sarong: A Malaysian wrap skirt. This long straight piece of fabric is traditionally hand-batiked with a deep fold in the front and held with a scarf that ties around the waist. This style has been borrowed and adapted to western fashion, first for beachwear and now for sportswear.

Saville Row: A West End street in London and the home of the finest English tailors. The customers are primarily wealthy international businessmen who value quality, custom service, and conservatism.

Secondary colors: Orange, green, and violet. Colors made by combining two primary colors: yellow and red make orange; blue and yellow make green; red and blue make violet.

Seasonless dressing: A dressing style made up of clothes that work regardless of the time of year; for example, a rayon dress.

Semiformal: Describing a dress code requiring a single- or double-breasted black suit for men, and evening or cocktail dress for women.

Separates: A retail term for sportswear items—skirts, jackets, blouses, and sweaters—that can be coordinated to wear together.

Silhouette: Literally, an outline; the lay of the material; the shape of the garment. In a broader sense, the forecast for trends in length and shape for the upcoming fashion season.

Slub: To allow the natural character of a fiber to show up in the surface of the weave.

Solid color: A single color without print or pattern.

Sportswear: Originally, clothing worn for active sports or for spectator sports. In the sixties, the term came to describe casual daytime clothes that reflected an informal lifestyle. Now "separates" and "sportswear" are interchangeable. The concept of modern sportswear is considered distinctively American.

Stone wash: Repeated washing of a fabric to fade the color; the effect of putting a stone in the washing machine with the clothes.

Stylist: A specialist who coordinates clothes and creates styles or looks; different from a designer.

Success dressing: Fashion with a yuppie influence for business or professional women; derived from men's fashion but softened with pleated skirts and feminine blouses.

Sweatclothes: Apparel worn for exercising and jogging, usually including shirts and pants in soft, absorbent materials.

Synthetic fiber: Chemically constructed filaments or fibers that are made from regenerated cellulose. They include nylon, rayon, vinyl, triacetate, spandex, saran, acrylic, and acetate.

Tailored: Fashioned or fitted; usually refers to men's styles. Tailored styles follow a set design and have enduring wearability.

Tartan: The specific plaid weave and coloration belonging to 18th-century clans or tribes in Scotland.

Textiles: General term for raw material and woven cloth.

Texture: Woven cloth or the character of the cloth.

Tiered look: A fashion for skirts and dresses composed of bands of gathered cloth.

Top: An item of clothing worn above the waist; for example, a blouse or a jacket.

Total look: The appearance evoked by wearing a unified, coordinated outfit.

Town wear: Street clothes.

Transparency: A texture so fine that it can be seen through. Gauzes and Georgettes are popular examples of transparent materials.

Tricolor: The red, white, and blue colors of the French flag.

Trompe l'oeil: Literally, to fool the eye. Usually applied to painting or—in the case of clothing—embroidery made to appear real.

T-shape: A design that stretches across the shoulders and tapers downward.

Tuxedo: A man's dinner jacket.

Glossary

Tweed: Rough wool cloth originally woven in Scotland; for jackets, pants, and skirts.

Twill fabric: The weave of this fabric shows a distinctive diagonal wale on the face of the fabric, as in denim or gabardine.

Twin prints: Two prints, such as a stripe and a dot, that share the same color combination. Twin prints are often used in the same garment.

Vogue: Fashionable. The fashion magazine *Vogue* reports designer trends to sophisticated consumers in French, British, American, Italian, Australian, and Japanese editions.

Vintage fashions: Used clothing and accessories from past fashion eras that are refurbished and sold as current fashion, usually in vintage markets or specialty shops.

Wardrobe: A planned assortment of clothes; a dresser or cabinet to store clothes in.

Warm colors: Colors with a red or yellow undertone and suggesting an energetic and upbeat image. The basic warm colors are red, orange, and yellow.

Waterproof: Impervious to water; can refer to clothing or cosmetics.

Wraparound skirt: One piece of material that wraps around the lower half of the body and fastens at the waist.

WWD: *Women's Wear Daily*, the Seventh Avenue newspaper published five days a week for retail and industry reporting on collections, government regulations, and foreign trade.

Yuppie: A Young Urban Professional; describing clothes worn by yuppies, whose annual income is said to be equal their age times $3,000. Legend has it that yuppies wear Ralph Lauren, Burberry, and Rolex watches; and they carry Gucci briefcases.

First published in the United States in 1992 by Chronicle Books.

Printed in Japan.

Library of Congress Cataloging-in-Publication Data

Dressing with color: the designer's guide to over 1,000 color combinations/[introductory essay by] Jeanne Allen.
p. cm.
ISBN 0-8118-0094-6 (pbk.)
1. Color in clothing. I. Allen, Jeanne, 1945– II. Shibukawa, Ikuyoshi. Color coordination 2.
TT507.D74 1992
646'.34—dc20
92-6820
CIP

Color Coordination 2 by Ikuyoshi Shibukawa and Yumi Takahashi was first published in Japan by Kawade Shobo Shinsha Publishers.

Translated by Kazu Morita
Edited by Terry Ryan
Cover design by David Alcorn

Distributed in Canada by Raincoast Books
8680 Cambie Street
Vancouver, B.C. V6P 6M9

10 9 8 7 6 5 4 3 2

Chronicle Books
275 Fifth Street
San Francisco, California 94103